how to create a
magical
home

how to create a
magical
home

marie bruce

quantum

LONDON • NEW YORK • TORONTO • SYDNEY

quantum

An imprint of W. Foulsham and Co. Ltd
The Publishing House, Bennetts Close, Cippenham, Slough,
Berkshire, SL1 5AP, England

ISBN 0-572-02963-2

The moral right of the author has been asserted

Cover photograph © The Image Bank

A CIP record for this book is available from the British Library

Neither the editors of W. Foulsham and Co. Ltd nor the author nor the publisher take responsibility for any possible consequences from any treatment, procedure, test, exercise, action or application of medication or preparation by any person reading or following the information in this book.

Printed in Great Britain by Creative Print & Design (Wales), Ebbw Vale

Contents

Dedication

For my mother, Jacqueline.
Thanks for picking me up when I fell,
in childhood and beyond.

With love from your Marianna xxx

Introduction

Did you know that by growing ivy up the walls of your house you can magically protect it from intruders? Or that when a rocking chair rocks by itself, someone is watching over you and protecting you? Did you know that standing a broom by your back door will invite the faerie folk into your home, that keeping goldfish can bring you prosperity, or that hanging a mirror over your bed can ward off bad dreams?

These are just some of the things witches do to protect and bring magic to their homes. Now you too can create and enjoy a truly magical home! Within the pages of this book are spells and rituals for every room in your house. Learn how to invoke the magical protection of household devas, how to grow magical herbs in the garden and blend potions in the kitchen. Discover how to choose colours, fabrics and fragrances that will turn your home into a haven of peace and tranquillity. Whether you live in a high-rise flat or a mansion, a bedsit or a bungalow, it really doesn't matter – there are things you can do today to bring the true essence of magic into your home and your life.

How to Create a Magical Home is a handbook for all those who want to get the most out of their living space. Here you will find protection spells, moving spells, cleansing rituals, household folklore and ways to create the essence of your dream home within the place where you live now. This book will ensure that you never look at your home in the same way again. It will guide you step by step and room by room as you make your home a magical space that works for you.

May your home be filled with magic and light!

Blessed be!

Morgana

A House of Magic

The witch's cottage is a staple of folklore and fairytale. Whether it be the gingerbread house that tempted Hansel and Gretal, or the enchanted tower that imprisoned Rapunzel, it plays a huge role in European folklore. Standing in the midst of a tangled forest, surrounded by a fragrant herb garden and well protected by thorny rose bushes and stone gargoyles, the witch's cottage both welcomes and repels us at one and the same time.

Those who dare to trespass in the garden may find a large toad sitting beside a pond, and a little wishing well with a wooden bucket that swings gently on creaking chains. The eyes of small creatures watch from the hedgerows as visitors make their way up the cobbled garden path towards the crooked cottage with its smoking chimney and windows of pretty coloured glass.

The heavy oak door is intricately carved with an oak-leaf design and is shaped like a Gothic arch. A sideways hung horseshoe is nailed above the point of the door. Beneath it a lion's face silently roars, daring anyone to rattle the knocker he protects. High up on the red-tiled roof stands a weather vane fashioned to look like a witch riding her broomstick through the night sky, and wind chimes hang from the eaves, filling the garden with their tinkling sound. An old broomstick decorated with ribbons and bells stands propped beside the door, and a black cat sits quietly on the step, waiting to be let in.

Inside the witch's cottage a log fire burns, filling the room with the scent of pine. A rocking chair stands before the hearth, and against the walls are armchairs covered with sumptuous velvet throws and cushions. Bowls of pot pourri give off the scent of summer roses, while faceted crystals, hung in the window, fill the room with dancing rainbows. Figures of witches proudly line the mantlepiece, and an oil-burner stands on the hearth. In one corner, a large pewter tree holds an array of flickering candles, and opposite it an altar has been set up ready for spell-casting. A thick Book of Shadows lies open on the carved wings of a dragon-shaped bookstand, and the light of the room is reflected in a large round mirror hung above the mantelpiece to represent the full moon.

In the kitchen a black iron cauldron stands ready on the stove. Gleaming copper pots and pans hang from a beam, together with bunches of herbs and flowers hung up to dry. Jars of herbs and bottles of potions line the kitchen walls; a mortar and pestle stand on the window sill; and a brass five-pointed star glints in the window above. An incense burner hangs from three chains in the corner, and a pretty jug of meadow flowers stands in the centre of the kitchen table.

A large woodcarving of a howling wolf guards the staircase. You go up the stairs to discover the bedroom scented with lavender, and pillows filled with mugwort to induce prophetic dreams. Protection charms hang from the bedposts, and a small altar dedicated to love and passion stands in the corner of the room. In the bathroom are rows of jewel-coloured lotions, potions and hair rinses. A pretty bowl is filled with sweet-scented soaps. The witch's cottage holds magic in every room, and every room of her home lends its power to her spell-castings.

Welcome to your magical home! If the description above has left you longing to live in the witch's cottage of old, then this is the book for you. Here you will discover how to turn your current home into your very own version of the fabled witch's cottage and how to create a magical sanctuary that not only aids your spell-castings but also nurtures your soul and protects you and your family from harm.

Some people believe that vast sums of money are needed to make a home beautiful, but this is really not the case. I realise that many of you reading this book will be living in situations that are far from your personal ideal – and that some of you will have come to this book out of sheer desperation! I know this because I too have lived in places that seemed to be in complete opposition to everything I wanted in life. But there are ways to make even the plainest house or bedsit into an attractive space with an uplifting atmosphere. And there are ways to create the essence of your dream home wherever you live now. In this book you will find things you can do today to make your home work for you and to attract all that you want in life. You can do these things even if you're a student living in a tiny bedsit, or a single mum living in a high-rise flat, or a council tenant living on benefits and struggling to make ends meet.

Even if you do have a great job, money in the bank and your own house, chances are there will be something missing from your home. Maybe it lacks a feeling of security, for example, or a sense of prosperity and general abundance. Maybe on the outside you appear to have everything, but your home is devoid of love, and the only passion you've experienced in a long time is a type of fruit!

Whatever your current circumstances and whatever your long-term goal, you will find techniques and concepts within this book that will help you to make the most of what you have right now while at the same time magnetising all that you truly want. What techniques am I talking about? Why, magic of course!

Magic

True magic is as natural as rainfall. We are all born with a spark of magic within us, and we all have personal power and a deep source of inner strength. The world around us is filled with the magic of nature and the power of the universe. Witches weave all of this together by calling upon our own magic and connecting it with nature. One way in which we do this is by carefully choosing the tools and symbols we use in spell-casting.

If you have read any of my previous books, you will already have a firm knowledge of how magic and spell-casting work. If you are new to witchcraft, much of what follows will be unfamiliar – but don't worry: all the spells in this book are simple to perform and positive in nature. You won't have to eat raw meat at midnight or dance naked at a crossroads under the full moon! What you will have to do is concentrate fully on whatever magical task you have in hand, as witchcraft will only work if you remain focused and visualise the required outcome of the spell clearly in your mind.

A HOUSE OF MAGIC

Magical tools

Before you start, you will need to collect a few simple witch's tools. As you can see from the list below, a witch's tools are very basic items that can be found in most modern kitchens, so don't wait until you can afford to buy custom-made Wiccan versions to get working; just raid your kitchen for suitable substitutes. In time you may decide to invest in a set of tools created specifically for the purposes of magic – and such items do help to create beautiful altars – but for now simply use whatever you have to hand. Your spells will be just as powerful, and, after all, this is exactly what the witches of old did, as they didn't have occult stores and New Age catalogues at their disposal!

Pentacle

The most important tool, a pentacle is a flat disc with a five-pointed star, known as a pentagram, inscribed on it. You can make one from clay, buy one from an occult store or draw one on card and cut it out.

Cauldron

This is a large heatproof vessel for mixing potions and burning fire spells, Wiccan cauldrons are available from occult stores but can be quite expensive. A large casserole dish or saucepan will do just as well for an alternative.

Chalice

A chalice is a stemmed drinking vessel used for taking potions. Pewter is the favoured material, but any stemmed drinking glass will do fine.

Athame

This is a ritual knife used for directing power and inscribing candles. Any paper knife or kitchen knife is suitable for this purpose.

Wand

Any fallen twig you come across can be used as your magical wand. Traditionally, a wand should reach from the tip of your middle finger to your inner elbow.

Broomstick

You can buy an old-fashioned twig broomstick, or besom, from most garden centres. These are used in magic to sweep away negative energy, for protection spells and for some faerie spells.

Creating a magical home

I've said it before, but I'll say it again: any home can be magical, regardless of how far from ideal it may seem. You do not have to move house to enjoy a magical home – although a move could well be part of your long-term plans. With a little time, effort and creative imagination, you can turn your current abode into a healing sanctuary that is full of positive magical energy. If you are Wiccan or on some type of magical path, you will find that all your spell-workings are greatly enhanced when you take the time to put magic back into your environment. If you are not currently a practitioner of magic, the ideas in this book will help you to make your home a relaxing and stress-free place to be – somewhere to cast off all your troubles and feel safe and nurtured.

Our homes are extensions of ourselves, so when we neglect them, we are actually neglecting ourselves. On some level we are saying, 'I am not worthy of a nice home.' This, of course, is simply not true – everyone deserves a calm and peaceful place that they can call their own, a place in which they can express themselves and be themselves fully. Take a few moments right now to think about how you treat your home. Do you vacuum regularly? Do you leave dirty dishes sitting in the sink? Does your home sparkle with cleanliness, or is there a thick layer of dust over everything? How does your home smell? Is it fresh and clean, or musty and stale? Do you take the rubbish out daily, or does refuse spill out on to the kitchen floor?

Be honest with yourself and you will see what needs to be done and where improvements can be made. Now, I'm not saying that you should spend every minute of the day cleaning the house – life is far too precious for that! But having a really good top-to-bottom clean and then keeping on top of things on a daily basis will help to create the beginnings of a magical home. The simple fact is that a magical home is a clean home – there's just no getting away from it! But there are ways to make cleaning more fun and more magical ...

Magical cleaning

In many cultures cleaning is an act of reverence and is done with a calm and meditative attitude. In the Western world we seem to have lost sight of the spiritual aspects of cleanliness and rely on throwing our clutter into cupboards ten minutes before visitors are due! However, there is incredible satisfaction in a good clear-out and a spring-clean that makes a home sparkle. Fortunately, there are many modern gadgets such as dishwashers, washing machines and vacuum cleaners to make housework less of a chore. In addition, we can learn how to put the magic back into our homes by cleaning in a magical way. Essential oils are great for this. By adding a few drops of the appropriate oil to our cleaning water we are actually making a magical cleansing potion. Good oils to try are grapefruit and lemon balm, both of which have uplifting qualities that will aid you in your chores. A few drops of grapefruit oil in your washing-up water will leave dishes sparkling and will help to energise you as you work. Many New Age stores sell specially blended magical washes that can be added to water in order to attract particular things to your life and your home. Prosperity washes, good luck washes, true love washes and many more are available, and could give you more of an incentive to brandish the mop and bucket!

A general rule when cleaning magically is to clean in an anti-clockwise, or widdershins, direction in order to banish the dirt. Another magical trick is to go around the house with a broomstick once all the vacuuming has been done. Hold the broom just above the floor and, again moving in a widdershins direction, quickly sweep any negativity out of the atmosphere, finishing by sweeping it out of the back door. This may at first seem a little silly, as the broom never actually touches anything but air; however, once you have completed the task you should notice that the house feels somewhat lighter and less oppressive. It's a good idea to repeat this process once a month, after the full moon.

The fragrance of your home is also important. A home that smells clean and fresh is inviting. Make sure you open the windows for at least an hour each day, or half an hour in the depths of winter. As you do so, ask the spirits of air to bless your house and all within. Finally, anyone interested in witchcraft will probably have a collection of incense sticks and cones, oils and oil-burners, scented candles and bowls of pot pourri scattered around the home. Each room requires a different fragrance, because each room has a different atmosphere – we will be exploring this subject room by room later in the book. For now, just keep your nostrils twitching for pleasant incenses and so on that will help you to create your magical home.

Getting rid of the clutter

Yes, you've heard it a million times before, I know, but a magical home does not resemble a junk shop! Not that I advocate the minimalist look, but there is good clutter and bad clutter. Good clutter is your CDs, books, videos, DVDs and treasured ornaments. Bad clutter includes old magazines and newspapers, impulse buys and family 'heirlooms' that no-one else wants! There's nothing like a good clear-out to really get the ball rolling with creating a magical home. When I have a clear-out I'm totally ruthless, and the more I chuck out, the better I feel! It's a great way to let go of the past and move forward in your life. Of course, this may be difficult if you're a hoarder, or if you cling to the past as if it's a life support system! But give it a go anyway. Get a stack of boxes for neatly storing the items that you choose to keep, plus a few old cardboard boxes to fill for charity shops – and lots of black sacks for the junk. You might also like to buy some bottles of mineral water, because this is thirsty work. Pick a day, put on some music and just go for it! Let go of the past and start moving forward into a bright new future in your magical home!

Cleansing and purification

Now that you have cleaned and de-cluttered your home physically, it's time to think about cleansing your space on a psychic level. Some people call this 'space clearing', others – including me – use the term 'cleansing and purification'. These are both basically the same thing – that is, a magical way of freeing the space of all negative energy. When our homes are filled with negativity, we can often feel lethargic and constantly exhausted. It is as if the weight of the negative energy is pressing down on us. This can affect our health, our relationships and any magic that we perform. Most witches and magical practitioners perform regular cleansings in their homes to keep their living space free of negativity, and the atmosphere light and welcoming. If the atmosphere of your home feels heavy and oppressive, chances are you need to perform a cleansing ritual.

A simple cleansing ritual

This quick and easy spell can be performed on a weekly basis if you wish, and should be done prior to any spells you cast within your home. It is also a useful way to clear the air after an argument between family members and will cleanse your home of negativity.

What you need
A little spring water, your chalice, ¹/₂ tsp sea salt

What you do
⭐ Open all the windows and invite the spirits of Air to bless and protect your home and those within.

⭐ Pour the spring water into your chalice and add the sea salt. Stir the potion with your index finger in a deosil, or clockwise, direction.

⭐ Beginning in the main room of your home, walk around deosil (clockwise), sprinkling the potion about with your fingers. As you do so, repeat these words:

> *By Earth and Water I cleanse this space.*

⭐ Go around the entire house, repeating this process in every room until all are cleansed. Pour any remaining potion down the drain and say:

> *Water of the ocean, salt of the sea,*
> *What is thine I return to thee.*

⭐ Play soothing music for a while and then go about your day.

A purification ritual

A purification differs from a cleansing in that each of the four elements is invoked separately, so by the end of the ritual you will have made four trips around your house. Purifications should be performed once a month on the new moon. You can also use this ritual if you move into a new home, after a divorce or separation or if you have recently been bereaved, as it will help to keep the energies around you positive.

In this ritual the sea salt represents the element of Earth, the spring water represents the element of Water, the candle or tea-light represents the element of Fire, and the incense represents the element of Air.

What you need
A small dish of sea-salt, a chalice of spring water, a white candle or tea-light in a suitable holder, a stick of incense in your chosen fragrance

What you do
⭐ Take up the dish of sea-salt and go around your home as described in the Simple Cleansing Ritual on page 16, purifying each room. As you make your trip, repeat these words:

> *By the sacred powers of the element of Earth, I do purify and protect this space.*

⭐ Now repeat this process with each of the other elemental representatives in turn, chanting the above words but substituting the appropriate element for 'Earth'.

⭐ When you have finished your purification, scatter the sea-salt to the winds, pour the spring water down the drain and allow the candle and incense to burn down naturally.

⭐ If possible, do something quiet for the rest of the day.

Altars

Altars are the one thing that is common to all witches' homes, although there are as many different altar set-ups as there are witches. The desire to create altars seems to be innate in most of us. We gather together photographs of loved ones and friends, we display a collection of favourite pictures or certificates on the wall, we arrange treasured possessions on dressers and in display cabinets. Even little children often have a collection that they take delight in arranging and re-arranging. These are all variations on the subliminal altar theme. Ideally, you should view your entire house and garden as one huge altar and a declaration of your magical ways. However, if you want a truly magical home, it is also essential to create some form of sacred altar within your personal space. Throughout this book we will be looking at different types of altar and considering how they relate to the various rooms of the house, what kind of magic they are best used for and what they can attract into your life. But for now let's take a look at a basic magical altar set-up.

A working altar is used for carrying out magical work. There are also altars dedicated to specific purposes, such as love, prosperity, health and so on; however, these are separate from the working altar. This altar should be large enough to hold all your magical tools and still leave enough space to work your spells. It should be sturdy and secure, as you will be placing burning candles and incense upon it. Traditionally, a working altar should be placed in either the north or the east of the altar room. This is because North is the direction of natural earth magic and East is the direction of new beginnings. Each spell you cast is actually a new beginning and opens a fresh page in your life.

Your main altar should be somewhere quiet and easily accessible. If privacy is a problem or you wish to keep your involvement in magic entirely to yourself, then a bedroom or study is an ideal place to set it up. If family and friends know of your interest or are of a like mind, then you might want your altar to be in a more communal room, such as the lounge, the kitchen or even the hallway.

The mantelpiece is a good place to set up a simple altar, as here three of the elements are present already – Fire (which is, of course, burning in the hearth – if only symbolically), Earth (which is the structure of the mantel itself) and Air (which is the ventilation of the chimney). In old houses the bedrooms often have a fireplace. This is the perfect spot for a private altar of some sort.

Once you have decided where your altar will be, clean the surface well, gather your tools together and arrange them attractively. Add a couple of white candles in tall candlesticks as illuminator candles, and a little incense or some oil and a burner. Place your broomstick and cauldron on the floor nearby. If you have a magic box filled with crystals, pendulums, tarot cards and so on, keep this near your altar too. Don't forget to personalise the space and perhaps introduce a magical theme by hanging crystals and wind chimes from the ceiling and putting up magical pictures, depicting, for example, the pentagram, the green man, fairies or leaves. Introduce a colour scheme and buy tools that co-ordinate. My own altar is filled with pewter. You might prefer cut glass, crystal, wood, terracotta or items that depict images of the sea. Finally, fill your chalice with fresh water every day to make sure your magical cup is always full and add a small bowl of sea salt or rock salt to complete the altar set-up. Remember that this is your altar, your space. Have fun with it and make it magical and individual to yourself. Take your time, as making this altar is the first step towards creating a truly magical home.

Household colour magic

Within the realm of magic, each colour holds a power of its own and is associated with a specific area of spell-casting. Part of creating a magical home lies in choosing colours wisely, not only for their ability to transform a room, but also for their ability to enhance a particular area of your life. For instance, my bedroom is decorated in deep shades of purple and pink. Pink is a very feminine colour and magically it attracts self-love, romantic love, friendship and nurturing. Purple is the witches' colour. It represents spell-casting, meditation, psychic awareness and prophetic dreams. It is also a colour of protection. As my working altar is in my bedroom, both these colours add their power not only to my magic but also to my life, my home and my general well-being. Below is a list of colours and their magical uses. Study them carefully so that you will be able to incorporate the correct colour magic for your needs into your magical home.

Red

Red is, of course, the colour of passion, love, lust and sex. It is also associated with danger, so too much red could become overpowering. It's a great accent colour for bedrooms and can help to increase love and passion if used in this area. As red is the colour of blood, it is associated with the divine feminine and with the gift of life itself. Red is a fabulous choice for rooms where lots of activity goes on or where much written work is done, as it stimulates the intellect. It is a good choice for studies, dining rooms and a powerfully passionate bedroom!

Pink

This is a gentle feminine colour that nurtures and protects. Pink is associated with self-love, friendship, romantic ideals, nurturing, youth and beauty. It's a great colour for girls and women of all ages, as it comes in so many shades. Little girls will love bubble-gum pink; sexy singletons may go for hot pink and cerise, toned down with candyfloss shades; and mature ladies may prefer the elegance of classic rose pink. This is a fabulous colour for both romantic and girly bedrooms, and accents of pink can also be used to great effect in sitting rooms and in bathrooms.

Orange

Orange is the colour of sociability and party time! As a solar colour, it is uplifting and creates feelings of happiness, cheerfulness and joy. It is great for rooms where families gather together, so pick shades of terracotta for your lounge or kitchen. Earthy oranges go well with deep wine-reds – if you're brave enough to put them together, that is!

Yellow

This is another solar colour. Yellow is pure sunshine and can look great in kitchens and bathrooms. Mellow yellow is nice for sitting rooms and reception rooms, as it helps to lift your spirits. Magically speaking, yellow can help to alleviate depression and is great for clarity of thought. Try sitting in a yellow kitchen with a mug of camomile tea to clear your mind and focus on whatever task you have in hand.

Green

Green is the colour that is easiest on the eye. It represents nature, growth, prosperity, fertility, abundance, career and the faerie realm. It is a gentle calming colour that comes in many shades and can attract wealth and prosperity into your life. As the colour of nature, it will also help you to attune with the natural world around you. Green is the perfect colour for transitional spaces such as hallways, conservatories, porches and reception rooms. Add lots of green plants to really show off this colour to its best advantage.

Blue

Blue is the colour of healing and harmony. As the colour that represents the element of Water, it has the ability to cleanse and purify. It is perfect for bathrooms, particularly in shades of aqua and turquoise. In its darker tones, blue is wonderful for creating a peaceful temple room or a restful bedroom. As the colour of the sky, it can uplift us and help us to reach new heights and aspire to greater things.

Purple

This is the colour of magic and witchcraft! Purple represents all aspects of psychic ability and spell-castings. It is a colour of gentle protection and will create an air of majesty and luxury wherever it is used. In the bedroom, purple will serve to enhance your dreams, so it is a great colour for those who are interested in dream interpretation.

Brown

As the colour of Earth, brown represents stability, neutrality and the animal kingdom. Brown and green together represent the immense powers of earth energy and can be used in the magical home to fill the house with universal magic. Creating a woodland theme will empower your home with the best of nature's strength and protection.

Black

Black is associated with banishing and binding spells, so it's the perfect colour for external doors and window frames, gates and garages. It will serve to protect your home and property on all levels. It is not a great colour for indoors, except for the odd curtain rail and wrought-iron candlestick, so use it to create accents.

White

White is, of course, the darling of the minimalists! White and ivory rooms can look great, but you must pay extra attention to the way you light and accessorise such rooms. Too much white can look stark and cold, or sterile and clinical. Off-whites, ivories and creams work well with rattan, leather and wood for a chic natural look. Lots of candles and cosy lamps will add a feeling of warmth.

Silver

Silver is a lunar colour and is associated with the divine feminine or Great Goddess. Magically, silver represents the moon and stars, night time, feminine power and abundance. It can be used successfully with purple, blue and white, and is a great colour for trimmings and accessories in most rooms.

Gold

Gold is a solar colour and is linked with the sun god and the divine masculine. In magic, gold represents the sun, daylight, summer time, masculine strength and abundance. Gold works well with most colours, especially red, orange, yellow and green. It is perfect for warming up a neutral decor and is, like silver, great for trimmings and accessories.

Dream Home

We all have a vision of our ideal home, the place we would escape to if we won the Lottery. For some, this is the archetypal cottage in the country; for others it is a super-modern apartment building in New York or London.

Whatever your dream home is, there is a strong chance that you began dreaming of it in childhood. Our childhood home has a strong and lasting effect on our psyche. If you lived in a small city house, crowded with parents and siblings and surrounded by bricks and concrete, you may dream of a home in the middle of nowhere, encircled by trees and greenery – a house where you could live in perfect peace and solitude with only your pets for company. Alternatively, you may not be able to imagine living anywhere except the city in which you were born. If you were an only child and spent much of your time home alone, your dream house may be a hive of activity, with people popping in and out all day long, offering you the company you craved as a child.

The things we are exposed to as children can also have an effect on our idea of a dream home. I remember once going slightly mad after a childhood trip to the circus – I made plans to run away and 'take to the sawdust', spending my life moving from place to place and riding horses under the big top! I even taught myself to juggle so that I would have an additional skill to offer! Although we generally grow out of our childhood passions, something of them always remains with us (I still juggle when I need to distract myself from daily life) and it is this that we can incorporate into our magical home.

So if you watched cowboy movies as a kid, maybe that explains your longing for a ranch-style house. If you spent family holidays on a caravan site, this could be the source of your secret desire to live the gypsy life! If you were fascinated by legends of mermaids and sirens, then it stands to reason that your dream home will overlook the sea. This may also be the case if you were drawn to tales of seafaring and smugglers – although in this instance your dream home may be on a boat. Perhaps your dream home is attached to a particular climate or country – a tropical beach hut for instance, a snowy Highland croft or an ice-covered log cabin in the Norwegian fjords. Whatever your ideal home is and wherever it is situated, it may seem as if there is a huge gulf between it and where you live now. And you may feel as if you will never bridge that gap – will never know the joy of living in your dream home. It's a very depressing thought. I know, because I used to feel like this too – until I discovered that my current home could be used as a magical tool to help me bring my dream home that much closer ...

Impossible princess?

My own dream home has been with me since earliest childhood. As I have grown up and moved on in my life, my dream home has evolved and developed too, but at its core it has always remained essentially the same. My dream home is the legendary fairytale castle that looks out over the sea and is protected by surrounding mountains and woodlands. It has turrets and towers covered in climbing ivy and briar roses. There is a stable block housing beautiful horses, and surrounding gardens filled with roses and sweet-smelling herbs. My castle also has something of a Gothic edge to it and is filled with medieval-looking furniture. Where has this idea come from? It is a fairytale vision that I first came across in childhood. My favourite

DREAM HOME

fairytales have always been 'Cinderella' and 'Sleeping Beauty', hence the rose-covered castle. I also loved 'Rapunzel', which explains the towers and turrets. Horses have always been a part of my life, so my dream home must accommodate them, and the witch in me needs herb gardens and a slightly spooky Gothic look to her home. As an incurable romantic, I love the Arthurian tales of knights in armour attending councils at the Round Table, so the medieval furniture would lend an air of Camelot to my home. All of which illustrates that my dream home is a combination of many aspects of my personality together with fond memories of childhood, and in all likelihood yours will be too, though the dream itself may be very different from mine.

Discovering your dream home

For this exercise you will need a pad, a pen and some quiet time alone. Light candles and incense if you wish, and perhaps have a glass of wine to help you to relax. Now get comfortable and close your eyes. You are going to ask yourself a simple and very empowering question, one that – if you answer it truthfully – will enable you to bypass any self-imposed limitations and discover what you truly want – what your soul needs. The question is: 'If I could have any home I wanted, what would it be?' Forgetting about practical considerations such as children, spouse or financial limitations, ask yourself that question now.

Really let your imagination run riot. Remember that there are no limits. Once you can see your dream home clearly in your mind, transfer that vision on to paper. Jot down what it looks like, how big it is, its location and surroundings, the views from the windows, the style of furnishings and so on. Are there any features that really stand out? Is there a garden, a loch or lake, the sea? What fragrances waft through your home? What sounds? Birdsong, children playing, the sound of horses munching on hay nearby? What plants and flowers are in and around your dream home? What colour is the decor? What textures surround you? Make your vision as evocative and as detailed as possible. The more work you do on it now, the easier it will be for you to transfer the essence of your dream home to the place where you live now.

Once you have a detailed description of your dream home, it should be relatively simple to discover the essence of the dream. The essence of my dream, for example, was the fairytale. Yours may be the same or it may be very different. Let's say your description included roses growing around the front door, the smell of baking bread in the kitchen and the sound of lambs bleating in the fields. In this case the essence of your dream home might be the country farmhouse. Let's say your description included the smell of saddle soap, the jingle of harness and the clinking of spurs, together with sculptures and paintings of horses in every room. Here, perhaps the essence of your dream is the ranch. Once you have extracted the essence from your dream, you have discovered the truth of your vision. And the truth can easily be re-created in your current residence to give you the experience of living in your dream home right now!

Why wait?

You don't need to wait until you win on Lotto to experience your dream home. Because the ideal home is a figment of our imagination, we carry it with us wherever we are. It is an extension of our soul. This means that we can bring the core of our soul home to our current home. Does this mean giving up on the dream? Absolutely not. It simply means that we can enjoy the essence of our dream home right now, instead of waiting until our circumstances or finances can bring us the real thing. There is a magical reason for taking this attitude, too. In the world of magic, like attracts like, so by creating the essence of your dream home right now, your current residence will magically begin to attract your dream home! You will also find that once you put your soul into your house it will begin to attract the items you need to re-create the dream.

Re-creating the dream

So how do you go about re-creating the essence of your dream home? It will seem much less daunting if you simply take one step at a time. This isn't a task that can be done overnight; it is a project that will take time and effort on your part. Let's imagine that your dream is the country farmhouse, but you live in a high-rise flat. Worlds apart? Yes. Hopeless? Not at all! Why not start by investing in a bread-making machine that will fill the flat with the farmhouse fragrance of newly baked bread? A CD of nature sounds that includes birdsong and lambs bleating will drown out the noise of traffic, and some rose trees in pots by the front door or out on the balcony will help to give a rural feel. Then you might like to decorate your flat with farmhouse pictures and statues of hens, cows and so on. Finally, try replacing take-away pizza with some good farmhouse-kitchen-style food and you will quickly feel your spirits lift.

What about the would-be rancher? She or he could decorate their home with pictures and statues of horses. Rosettes and horse brasses will also add to the ranch-style atmosphere, as will anything vaguely 'cowboy' – stetsons, cowboy boots, coils of rope, saddlery, cowhide rugs and so on. Play country music and take riding lessons; you will soon feel that your dream is much closer.

In taking these simple steps we are putting a little of our soul into our current environment and, in turn, our effort will magically attract more of the dream. I realise that this may be hard to believe, but it really does work. I know it works because I'm surrounded by my dream as I write. Remember my fairytale castle? The essence of that dream exists within my current home. Every night I retire to a Sleeping-Beauty-style four-poster bed. Hand-painted wrought-iron roses 'grow'

up the side of the bedroom door, just as they did over Sleeping Beauty's chamber. A glass slipper stands on the dressing table, and a red velvet witch's cloak hangs by the altar, looking for all the world as if it was left there by Red Riding Hood! A statue of Lancelot lends strength, honour and romance to my home, while the chaise longues are draped with medieval-style canopies that bring an air of Guinevere's elegance and the splendour of Camelot. I have the beginnings of a Gothic staircase, complete with Egyptian mummy sarcophagus, gargoyles, vampires and wolves. My riding hat and boots stand close by, reminding me that my horses are never really far away and are an important part of my life.

None of this has happened overnight; it has taken a lot of time and hard work to put it all together. But each item brings the dream closer and in its turn seems to magnetise some other aspect of the fairytale to my house. I am fully convinced that when my house is finished and every room reflects my dream home, then I'll discover my own miniature turreted house – my fairytale castle!

Go back to your own description of your dream house. What can you do today that will capture a little piece of the essence? What can you do tomorrow, next week, next pay day? Make a list of ways you can re-create something of your ideal home and steadily work your way through them. It may be something as simple as dining on French bread, strong cheese and fine wine to capture your French château; or it could be turning up the heating on your day off and taking a siesta as you would in your Spanish villa. Alternatively, it could mean learning a new skill. If your dream home is a ski lodge, you might want to take lessons on a dry ski slope. If you want to live in the frozen lakes of Norway, learn how to skate at your local ice rink. Get the idea? Do something today, however small, that will immediately capture something of your soul home.

Dream home book

Another way to attract your dream home is to create a dream home book. This is especially effective if you are short of cash and are finding it difficult to buy the things you need to re-create the dream in your current home. You can spend many a happy evening working on the book or just flicking through it and allowing yourself to escape for a while. I firmly believe that everyone should have a dream home book. It will lift your spirits when you feel low, and keep your thoughts positive and your mind on track with your long-term goal. Again, a dream home book requires that you spend time on it, and will grow and develop in a gradual way.

The first step is to find an attractive book with blank pages. An A4 hard-bound book is ideal. A scrapbook is also suitable but won't be as durable. Alternatively, you could use blank pages, poly pockets and a ring-binder. Once you have your book, turn to the first page and write 'My Dream Home' at the top. Now copy the notes you made for the Discovering Your Dream Home exercise on pages 25–6 so that you have a complete and detailed description of your soul home. If you are artistic, you might also like to draw a picture of the house you aspire to live in one day.

Next write down a detailed description of a typical day in your dream home. Living in your ideal home is inextricable from living your ideal life as well, so use this exercise to do some goal-setting. For example, if you have aspirations to become a writer, make a note of what proportion of your day is spent in the study writing. You could even write down the name of the publishing house you write for. If you plan to learn to ride or own a horse, incorporate riding time into your dream home day. If you want to spend your evenings relaxing in the conservatory with a glass of wine, then jot this down too. Think in terms of a lifestyle as well as just the home itself, and try to make your description as realistic and detailed as possible.

The next step is to go through old magazines and catalogues and cut out any pictures that suggest what you want in your ideal home or fit the lifestyle you are planning. For instance, the would-be writer might add pictures of desks and computers. The would-be rider might cut out pictures of their dream horse or of a model in full equestrian gear. If you dream of sleeping in a four-poster bed, find a picture of one and glue it into your book. This is what I did. It took a year for the real thing to manifest, but manifest it did! This goes for any other items of furniture you desire. Add fabric swatches and colour pallets so you have a representation of the decor. If you want a particular plant or flower in the garden, staple in a packet of the appropriate seeds. Try to make this book represent every aspect of your ideal home and lifestyle.

Finally, make sure you look through the book on a daily basis. As you do so, say to yourself, 'I will have all of this and more – it is all coming to me.' Keep the book on or near your altar to enhance its magical energies and know that you have taken the first step towards manifesting your dream home and your ideal life.

Dare to dream

Many people are so wrapped up in the day-to-day grind that they rarely take the time to day-dream. Magical day-dreaming is a very powerful and effective technique that can be used to magnetise all that you want into your life. Like attracts like, and our subconscious doesn't know the difference between fantasy and reality! We can use this to our advantage. If we spend just a few minutes each day focusing on what we want, we can attract our heart's desire. Magical people spend a lot of time day-dreaming, but we do it in a particular way. Most people frame their dreams in a negative way, saying to themselves: 'I'm so far from where I want to be! I'm never going to get what I want.' Magical people take a different approach. We use our day-dreams as an affirmation of success. In other words, we imagine what we want as if we already have it, saying to ourselves, 'I can have this and more.'

Witches call this magical day-dreaming 'visualisation', and we use it to attract good things into our lives. We add spell-work and ritual to reinforce our visualisations, but never a day goes by when we do not acknowledge how far we've come and how close we are to all we want. And the fantastic thing about this magical technique is that you can do it anywhere and no-one need know what you're up to! Start today and spend a few moments imagining yourself into your ideal life.

Spell to magnetise your dream home

When you have done as much as you can to bring the essence of your dream into your current home, try this spell to bring you a real fairytale castle, cowboy ranch or whatever your dream may be. It will help to draw your dream home towards you so that it will manifest within your life. Start to magnetise your dream home right away, regardless of your current circumstances, as magic will always find a way! You should work the spell every full moon.

What you need
A birthday cake candle in a holder

What you do

⭐ When the moon is full, light the birthday candle and say:

I magnetise my dream home into my life.
I pull it towards me in ways I do not yet know.
It is coming to me.

⭐ As the candle burns, speak the following chant:

Dream home, come to me,
Whether it be across land or sea.
Dream home, come to me;
This is my will; so mote it be!

⭐ Blow out the candle, as you do so, making a final wish for your dream home.
⭐ Every night before you go to sleep, spend time visualising yourself living in your dream home.

Your dream home will come to you, but if your dream is elaborate, you may have to be patient. If you have a big imagination and want more than the average house, you may have to be prepared to wait more than the average time. But in the end our dreams do come true when magic is behind us. It will be well worth the wait!

Household Spirits

The witch's cottage is full of household spirits. As she goes about her daily chores and magical activities, she will consistently acknowledge the magical beings who grace her home and bestow their gifts of power on her work. She will thank the elemental brownie for protecting her cauldron, light a candle to honour the ancestral witches of her bloodline, give thanks to the land deva for protecting the property and invoke the weather gifts of the four major elementals – be it a heavy rainfall to keep away unwanted visitors, or a strong breeze to dry the washing on the line. She will ask the angels to fill her home with love and light, and request that the pixies bring joy and laughter to herself and her guests. Statues of the goddesses Hestia and Vesta stand on the hearth and the household altar, bringing the very essence of magic and women's wisdom into her home.

We can all learn something from this traditional form of British witchcraft, and we can repeat such acts of reverence in our modern homes to bring in the essence and power of the witch's cottage. To recapture the power of household spirits is relatively easy; however, you will need to be able to keep an open mind and accept that much of childhood folklore has an underlying basis of truth. Though you may at first scoff at the very idea of brownies and pixies, witches have been using these elemental powers for centuries. Every hearth and home has its household spirits, and though they may have become lazy and inactive due to neglect, they can be reactivated by using the powers of the Craft. This means that you can effectively invoke a whole army of household spirits to protect your home and property; guard your loved ones; and fill your house with love, light, laughter and, of course, magic!

Learning how to communicate and work with household spirits is a fundamental key to re-creating the essence of the witch's cottage within your own home. And such spirits can help you to magnetise your dream home too. But before you can invoke the power of these beings, you need to know who and what you're dealing with, so read on ...

Classical goddesses

The classical mythologies of Greece and Rome contain two main figures of hearth and home. Their names are Hestia and Vesta. These powerful goddesses are the guardians of the household, bringing protection, security, love and abundance to our abodes. Both the Greek Hestia and the Roman Vesta were virgin goddesses. In its ancient context the word 'virgin' means simply 'beholden to no man, complete in herself, needing no other'. Witches hold true to this deeper meaning of the word, and virgin goddesses are revered as much for their strength and fierce independence as for their magical powers. So while Hestia and Vesta were the creators of the home, they certainly weren't down-trodden housewives or doormats for the menfolk to walk all over! They were powerful women in their own right.

These goddesses were true housewives, taking pride in the smooth running of the home, instilling their magic into their calm abodes and receiving honour and respect for doing so. Vesta and Hestia are true role models for today's busy women, going methodically about their business of nest-building and home-making. They can teach us an attitude of unruffled calm and detachment – what doesn't get done today will be done tomorrow. No stress, no panic, just a methodical routine of little and often, coupled with a few moments of spell time each day to keep the magic flowing. It is as important to these goddesses to enjoy their home as to create and maintain it.

Many modern witches call on Aphrodite for her gifts of love and beauty. Others call on Demeter for her assistance through the trials of motherhood. Very few call on Vesta and ask for help with the housework! But this is exactly what we should all be doing. By spending just a few moments concentrating on Vesta and her powers, you will find that she puts a spring in your step and joy in your heart as you drag out the ironing board or vacuum the stairs. She may inspire you to play a particular type of music as you clean, and this in turn will energise you and help get the job done more quickly. A scented candle while dusting? A cool glass of wine while ironing? Why not? Just because housework has to be done, it doesn't mean that you cannot gain any pleasure for yourself while doing it.

Before you begin your next cleaning job or household chore, close your eyes for a moment and call Vesta's name three times. Then light a tea-light, pop it in an appropriate holder, such as a decorative lantern, and place this on the hearth – the area of the home most closely associated with this powerful goddess. And finally, anyone who makes their living cleaning homes, offices, hospitals, hotels and so on should regard Vesta as a personal guardian. She will help you to find more satisfaction in your work and thus make your job more rewarding in the long run.

Lares

The lares are the classical guardians of the storeroom. They are also thought to be linked to family ancestors. In the magical home they should be called upon to ensure that there is always enough food in the cupboards and that the fridge-freezer remains well stocked so that want isn't felt. Again, the simple act of lighting a candle and stating your wish that the lares protect you and yours from need will be sufficient, but remember to repeat this power wish regularly. The best time for this is on the day of your shopping trip, when you fill the cupboards anew. Don't forget to give thanks for all you've already received.

Elementals

Elementals are the magical energies of nature. Known also as faeries or the fey, these beings preside over the weather and the growth of plants, trees and crops, and are generally regarded as the magical guardians of the planet. There are many types of elemental, including brownies and pixies, and they can be divided into two groups: major and minor elementals. There are four types of major elemental; they are the gnomes, the sylphs, the salamanders and the undines. The minor elementals include the brownies, the pixies and the land devas. These 'minor' beings are in fact very powerful in their own right. They often work in conjunction with one of the major elemental groups, thus offering a great source of magical strength to you and your home.

Gnomes

Associated with the element of Earth and the direction of North, gnomes can assist with the security of your home and are excellent guardians. It's no accident that many British gardens are filled with representations of these powerful beings, as they will protect the home that they are attached to. Gnomes can also be called upon to bring financial stability to your home, attracting the funds needed to pay a bill or to meet an emergency expense.

Sylphs

Associated with the element of Air and the direction of East, sylphs are faerie-like beings who govern the clouds and the winds. They can be called upon to bring a good breeze on washing day, or to make a gale or thunder storm move swiftly past your home without causing damage. Sylphs can also be invoked to improve communications between family members and to bring general blessings to your home.

Salamanders

Associated with the element of Fire and the direction of South, salamanders are small fiery dragon-like creatures that reside in every flame, beam of sunlight and flow of electricity. They can be tricky creatures to work with because of their fiery nature – fire can be beneficial or destructive, and it can easily get out of hand. It is vital that you state your need for non-destructive fire energies before working with these beings. Having said that, the magical home just wouldn't be the same without these feisty little spitfires. We use the power of salamanders more often that we are aware, for where would any modern witch be without her hair dryer and straightening irons? Witches who use candle magic and fire spells a good deal, soon get to know the power of the salamanders. Magically speaking, the salamanders can offer the strongest form of elemental protection, especially via their larger cousins, the dragons. They can also bring love and passion to your home, and can even guard it against lightning strikes and accidental fire. This is definitely an elemental you want on your side, but do tread carefully, as salamanders can sometimes be a bit unpredictable!

Undines

Associated with the element of Water and the direction of West, undines are gentle water sprites. Their family includes mermaids and sirens. In nature they govern the tides and the rains, the mists and the fogs, as well as acting as guardians of rivers, streams, lochs, lakes and oceans. Magically, the undines can help with cleansing, healing, understanding emotions, and dream rituals, so they often feature in the bathrooms and bedrooms of magical homes. Calling the seductive sirens in particular can increase your powers of allure, so include a representation of one in your bedroom if sexiness is what you're after.

Brownies

Brownies are minor elementals who work closely with the gnomes. Traditionally, a brownie is a small almost sloth-like creature covered in soft brown hair – hence his name. In folklore, he generally lives behind the oven. Magically, brownies are the helpers of the family, and work to ward off danger. Their main job within the magical household is to guard the sacred cauldron, allowing none to tamper with this powerful tool. They can also be called upon to protect all magical altars within the home. In days gone by, a witch would leave offerings on the kitchen table for her household brownie to enjoy while she went off to her sabbat meetings. This tradition is still carried on by children today every Christmas Eve, when they leave a glass of sherry and a mince pie for Santa, along with a juicy carrot for Rudolph.

Offerings should be left overnight so that your brownie can take his psychic fill, and the physical remains should be buried in the garden next morning. Tradition states that brownies prefer fresh milk and a sweet cake to anything else. It is also said that should you accidentally drop food on the floor anywhere in your house, you should leave it for a moment and then place it on your table or altar that night as an offering, for it now belongs to your household brownie.

Pixies

Pixies are the smaller cousins of the more powerful elves. They work closely with the sylphs to bring about good communication among family members. Within the magical home their job is to bring joy, fun, frolic and laughter. They can be called upon to make a dinner party go with a swing and will help to make sure everyone has a good time at any party you hold. The pixies place themselves wherever family and friends like to gather, so dining rooms and kitchens tend to be their favourite place of residence. They can be a little mischievous and like nothing better than to hide things away – and then make them re-appear in a totally different place a few weeks later!

Land devas

Land devas are powerful entities who work closely with all other elementals attached to your home and the immediate surrounding area. Whenever a building is constructed, the deva of that land will either extend her protection to encompass the new building and those within or, in some cases, work to sabotage the building process in order to preserve the land. In this sense, devas are nature's own eco-warriors! Once you have made contact with your household deva, you will be able to invoke her assistance with any number of spells, rituals or mundane problems – and working with these beings can be very rewarding. Their energies can be harnessed to bring a strong feeling of protection and security to your home, making you feel as safe as if you lived in a castle or huge stronghold. They have the ability to scare away unwanted visitors, door-to-door salesmen, debt collectors, bailiffs and people of a criminal intent. In short, your household deva can keep away anyone you would not wish to see and can protect you and your home from those who mean you harm.

This type of elemental is especially good for those living in blocks of flats or crowded housing estates, as it offers a protection that magically separates your home from all those around it. Devas can also be called upon to deal with disagreeable, unsavoury or dangerous neighbours, as they will only accept people who are conducive to the peace and harmony of the area. They are thus invaluable to those who are forced to live in close proximity to strangers or, shall we say, 'bad company'! Crime is a fact of life in every town and city in Britain, but your household deva can protect you from it. First, though, you must make her welcome into your life.

Honouring the deva

The first step to working with your household deva is to honour her and welcome her into your home and your life. As the deva is closely associated with nature, the best way to gain her attention is through gathering together a few beautiful green plants.

What you need
Some attractive green pot plants, some crystals, some sticks of incense

What you do

⭐ Arrange the pot plants together attractively in your home and place the crystals on the top soil to create a natural altar.

⭐ Dedicate this altar to the deva by saying the following words, or similar ones of your own choosing:

> *Deva of the land, gracious elemental, I bid you welcome to my home. I place here these beautiful plants that you may always have a place to rest within these walls. I honour your presence and ask for your protection. Blessed be!*

⭐ Burn a stick of incense here on a daily basis, saying as you light it:

> *Household deva, I honour you and give you thanks for your continued protection. Blessed be!*

⭐ Stake the incense into the soil and leave it to burn down.

Invoking the land deva

Sometimes we may need to do more than simply honour the land deva's presence. We may need to make a specific request and invoke her powers. This could be because we feel threatened in some way and feel the need for her protection and renewed vigilance with regard to our safety, or it could be that we are having trouble with a neighbour and would like to banish the negative energy that surrounds the relationship. Whatever the precise nature of the problem, if it revolves around home and security, your household deva can help.

What you need

Your athame (if you have one), candles and incense for the altar

What you do

⭐ Go to your main working altar and, using your athame, cast a magic circle by holding the blade out in front of you and turning three times deosil (clockwise). If you don't have an athame, simply use your index finger. In your mind's eye, envision the circle around you as electric blue light.

⭐ Light the candles and incense on your altar.

⭐ Breathe deeply three or four times, then stand with your feet shoulder-width apart and raise your arms high above your head, palms facing forwards. This is the gesture of invocation. Concentrate on the powers of your household deva and invoke her energies with the following charm:

> In this right and ready hour
> I call upon an ancient power.
> Here now I stand alone
> To welcome the land deva into my home.

⭐ You may feel a slight change in temperature or a shiver down your spine. This means that the land deva is with you and is listening. Tell her your troubles truthfully and make your request, then bow your head in thanks.

⭐ Take down the magic circle by turning three times widdershins (anti-clockwise). Imagine the blue light being drawn back into the athame or your finger.

⭐ Blow out the candles and go about your day knowing that the deva is now aware of your problem and will begin to help you through it.

Ancestors

In many cultures across the globe the ancestors are welcomed into the home and the lives of the present generation. Honouring those of our bloodline who have gone before is a way of connecting with the Otherworld and of coming to terms with the passing of time and our own mortality. Nothing lasts forever, and we must all pass through the gates of birth and death.

In general, there are two types of ancestor – ancient ancestors and immediate ancestors. Our ancient ancestors are those far back in the depths of time, while our immediate ancestors are our grandparents, uncles, aunts, parents and so on – people we knew in life or were told stories of by an older generation. Just as we all have two biological parents, so we also have two ancestral lines, and we may feel a stronger pull from one direction or the other, although this will generally balance itself out in one way or another. For example, I have always felt closer to my maternal line with regard to immediate ancestors. However, the strongest pull from my ancient ancestry comes through my paternal bloodline of Clan Bruce.

Ancient ancestors are usually the ones who bring great strength and courage in times of trouble, while our immediate ancestors bring comfort and consolation. Both can offer protection and guidance.

A traditional way to welcome your ancestors is to set up a small shrine. This doesn't have to be a morbid space draped in black velvet. It can simply be a joyful collection of photographs and mementoes gathered together to welcome the presence of our ancestors into our life and home. Such a shrine can also help us to come to terms with our culture and background. For instance, although I currently live in England, my ancestors pull me towards Scotland, and my first visit there was a true homecoming. I know that one day this pull will become so strong that I will relocate, but for now I honour my bloodline with a small shrine of figures fashioned after Scottish heroes. I also try to visit Scotland as often as I can to reconnect with the land and the culture, both of which are very different from those of England and the English.

Britain is a multi-cultural society and many of you reading this book will have far wider cultural differences to reconcile than I do, perhaps regarding a far-off land as your true home or a significant part of your heritage. An ancestral shrine can help you to maintain a connection with your homeland no matter how far away it may be, while at the same time empowering the home you live in now with ancestral protection and the power of your hereditary culture.

Angels

Angels are celestial beings that transcend all cultures and religions. In other words, they can be called upon by absolutely anyone, whatever their faith or religious beliefs. Angels are beings of light and love. They are here to help us and to protect us. There's only one condition: they are not allowed to intervene in human lives unless we ask them to. And how many people do you know who go around asking the angels for help? The angels are a neglected source of assistance. We all have a guardian angel who is just waiting to be of assistance to us. This incredible source of goodness and power is willing to guide us on our true path, protect us from harm and love us unconditionally. All we have to do is open our hearts and our minds and acknowledge its presence.

Fortunately, angels are masters of telepathy and can take the subtlest of hints! This means that something as simple as wearing an angel pin can open up the channels of communication. The silent plea 'Guardian angel, help me now!' will be heard and acted upon. Angels have a great sense of humour, and no job is too big or too small for them, so if you're looking for a gardener or a plumber, ask your angel to help you find one who is competent, reliable and won't rip you off! Can't get the lid off the pickle jar? Ask your angel to give you strength – trust me, it works!

Angels are invaluable to the magical home, and their energies can fill your house with an atmosphere of harmony and tranquillity. Calling on the angels after a family argument can help to restore peace, prompting an apology and reconciliation. The energies of the angels will also help you to magically create the kind of place you want to live in, assisting you in re-creating the essence of your dream home. Working with angels will, in addition, give your spells an added boost of power and will ensure that your work harms none, in accordance with the laws of magic and the Wiccan Rede: 'Do what you will and harm none'.

To invite the presence of the angels into your home, invest in a lantern or candlestick with an angelic design and burn candles in it regularly. If you would like to open up the channels of communication immediately, then perform the following simple ritual.

To commune with angels

If you want to use an angel representation for this ritual, bear in mind that Christmas is the best time of year for angel shopping, as Christmas cards and decorations are a good source of angel images.

What you need

A white candle and a suitable holder, a vase of white lilies, a representation of an angel (optional)

What you do

⭐ Set the candle, the vase of lilies and the angel representation (if you are using one) on an appropriate surface – your working altar is ideal – and settle before it comfortably.

⭐ Breathe deeply for a few moments, then light the candle and say the following words (or ones of your own creation):

> *I light this candle in honour of the angels. I ask the angels to fill this home with love and light and to assist me in my endeavour to create a magical home and healing sanctuary for myself and my family. May the angels guard and protect this home and all within. So mote it be! Blessed be!*

⭐ Remain at the altar for a short while, contemplating the powers you have invoked. If you have a specific request to make, make it now.

⭐ Let the candle burn for as long as you are in the room, then blow it out and continue with your day.

As you can see, there are elementals and household spirits to suit all affinities and magical abilities. There is no limit to the number of household spirits you can work with. During the course of this book we will be casting spells with all of them as we work our way through the rooms of the magical home.

Doors of Power

Doors and windows are the eyes of our homes. From them we can look out onto the world, and through them the world can look in at us! As portals between one realm and another, doors are symbolic of transition, and may also function as devices of protection.

The exterior of your home can say many things about who you are, your personality and how you want the world to see you. We have only to think of the phrase 'keeping up with the Joneses' to realise that how our home is perceived by others is very important to us. For some people the exterior of their house is very much a status symbol – a sign to the outside world that they are successful in their work and financially stable. Such people may take a pride in ensuring that the exterior of their house is immaculately presented. Having a perfectly trimmed hedge, a beautifully mown lawn and the right kind of car on the drive will probably be very important to them.

Sadly, however, a pristine exterior may be an invitation to those with criminal intent. Most of us know someone who has been burgled or have ourselves experienced a break-in. Such an invasive experience can be very harrowing and difficult to come to terms with, leaving us feeling vulnerable and open to attack. In some inner-city areas it may be wise to keep the exterior of your home a little understated, saving your status-symbol purchases for inside the house. Of course, this doesn't mean that you can't have anything nice, just that you keeep your treasured possessions indoors and out of sight, and that the exterior of your house is nice and tidy but not flashy.

We will be looking throughout this chapter at magical ways to protect your doors and windows, but for now I'd like you to go outside and look at your house through the eyes of a would-be burglar. How easy would it be to break into your home? Do all the doors and windows have secure locks? Do you close all windows before leaving the house – some burglars have been known to pose as window cleaners (carrying their own ladder), while others pretend to be removal men and calmly carry your TV and stereo into their waiting van. Imagine for a second that you have lost your key and are locked out. How would you get in? If you could get in, then an intruder could too. One of the first things magical students learn is that all magic must be backed up by practical actions in the everyday world. This means that before you work any of the spells in this chapter, it is in your own interests to have window locks, door chains, dead bolts and an alarm properly fitted. You already know this, of course, but how many of you can actually say that your home is as secure as you can possibly make it? While magic does go a long way towards protecting us and keeping us safe, it cannot prevent a thief walking in through an unlocked door or stealing your purse through an open window. Be smart, be vigilant, be safe.

Threshold magic

The threshold is considered to be magical in its own right, since it must be crossed in order to enter the building. Many superstitions have grown up around this part of the home. For instance, it is thought that if a groom carries his bride over the threshold of the marital home, the marriage will be a long and happy one.

On New Year's Eve it is traditional for a member of the family to go outside at 11.59 p.m. and wait until midnight has struck. At this point the family members will open the door and invite him back in; thus he takes out the old year and brings in the new. Placing a shiny silver coin on the threshold on New Year's Eve and bringing it in at midnight is said to bring prosperity throughout the coming year. The coin must not be spent though, but buried in the garden the following New Year and a new one placed on the threshold. On New Year's Day we have the tradition of 'first footing', in which the first person to cross the threshold should be a dark-haired man carrying a piece of coal. In days gone by, coal was a source of wealth, and it still represents luck and good fortune. This tradition, however, has largely faded into the practice of taking a gift to the first house you visit in the New Year –

bottles of wine are very popular for this purpose. If you want to hold true to the old tradition but haven't got any coal, you could take a charcoal block designed for burning incense instead.

In folklore, a vampire cannot cross the threshold of a building without first being invited in – a superstition that echoes the belief in the protective properties of the threshold and the doorway in general. In Celtic tradition it was believed that to bury an item of metal beneath the threshold would keep the faeries out and prevent them making mischief. Witch bottles (see page 63) would be placed on the threshold to keep away evil spirits.

To make your own threshold more magical, place a couple of miniature holly trees in planters by each side of the door. Holly is a very protective plant and is sacred to the Horned God of witchcraft. You could add to this protection by growing ivy up the external walls and around the doorway. Ivy is another plant of strong protection and will also bring good luck to the home it grows upon. To keep away unwelcome visitors, place a statue or wall plaque by the threshold. Gargoyles, lions and dragons can all be found in garden centres and are traditional threshold guardians, while a Green Man plaque will invoke the protection of the witches' god.

To protect the threshold

What you need
A mortar and pestle, 2 tsp dried rosemary, 3 tsp dried marigold petals, a statue of your chosen guardian (optional)

What you do
- Place the rosemary and marigold (both of which have strong protective powers) in the mortar and grind them into a fine powder using a deosil (clockwise) direction.
- Once the herbs are finely ground, hold your hands palms down over the mortar and say:

> *May these powerful herbs serve to protect the sacred threshold of my magical home. So mote it be!*

⭐ Wait until the witching hour and, on the stroke of midnight, scatter the herbs on and around your threshold, as you do so saying:

> *Protected be!*

⭐ To enhance this spell, scatter a few of the herbs over the statue of your chosen guardian and place it on your doorstep.

To ward the doorstep

If you have a step or steps to your home, you might like to perform this spell to keep intruders away and to prevent nasty accidents from happening to you or your loved ones – steps can be especially dangerous to children and the elderly. If you're worried about what the neighbours will think, this spell will be only enhanced if you perform it at midnight!

What you need
A piece of white chalk

What you do
⭐ Using the chalk, in each corner of the first step draw a small pentagram, or five-pointed star.
⭐ Next, draw a line at the very base of the step – where it meets the next step or the pavement.
⭐ Now place both hands palms down on the step and say the following charm:

> *Let my loved ones pass by with harm to none*
> *But trip the intruder and let him be gone!*
> *So mote it be!*

⭐ Work your way up the steps, drawing the pentagram and the line and chanting the charm on each one.

Doors

As already mentioned, doors are portals between spaces; however, this does not only mean between the inside and outside of a building. A door can also be a portal to another realm. For example, in the book *The Lion, the Witch and the Wardrobe* the way into Narnia is through a wardrobe door, while in the TV series *Doctor Who* the door to the tiny police phone box opens into the vast expanse of the Tardis. These are magical doorways indeed!

Superstition warns that we should always face the door as we close it or misfortune will stalk us, while a door that does not face onto the street is thought to be unlucky. It is also said that leaving internal doors slightly ajar will invite ghosts to take up residence in your home. Slamming doors was once believed to trap evil spirits. Maybe this is why some of us slam doors when we are annoyed, in an unconscious effort to trap the evil spirit of our anger!

Perhaps the most magical and protective doorway is the drawbridge of ancient castles. This was usually crafted in oak and was let down to enable visitors to cross the moat – thus passing over the element of Water and across the sacred threshold in one go. A portcullis was often added to increase the security of the castle. It was usually made of iron to guard against the fey or faerie folk, who hated such metals.

Doors have always been first and foremost a protection device, keeping out unwanted visitors and yet swinging wide in welcome for our chosen guests. While today we do not have the safety and security of the drawbridge, there are still many things we can do to magically protect the doors of our homes.

Knock on wood

While many modern homes are fitted with glazed, semi-glazed or UPVC doors, a door of solid wood offers the greatest magical protection and is most in keeping with the witch's cottage of old. Wood, however, has a symbolism of its own. If your door is made of one of the woods listed on page 49, this will go a long way towards enhancing the energies of your magical home.

Oak

For centuries this was the most commonly used wood for doors. Its density not only offered protection but also helped to keep the heat inside draughty castles and manor houses. Magically speaking, oak symbolises strength, protection, resistance, resilience and great wisdom. Interestingly, in the Celtic Ogham the word for oak is *duir*, which means 'door'. This wood is sacred to Herne the Hunter, Robin Hood and the Oak King, who presides over the summer months and the light half of the year.

Pine

Pine is the modern choice of wood for most builders and joiners. It is cheap and easy to buy, and is strong enough to offer protection as an external door yet attractive enough to be used internally too. In a magical sense, pine represents purification, prosperity, creativity, healing and abundance.

Ash

If your door is made of ash, it is magical indeed, as ash is the wood of Yggdrasil, or the World Tree, which links the three realms of the Otherworld, our own world and the Underworld. This is reflected in the way a door links the two worlds of the internal and external.

Cedar

Cedarwood is symbolic of the Otherworld, so a cedarwood door really is a door to other worlds. Cedarwood is symbolic of wisdom, clarity of thought and inspiration.

Protection of doorways

If your door is not made of any of the above woods – or of wood at all – don't despair. There are many ways to enhance the protective powers of any door.

- ✪ An age-old protection device is to tie two yew twigs together with red ribbon, so that they form an equal-armed cross. This should be hung high above your front door and will guard you from all evil, both worldly and Otherworldly.

- ✪ Placing a pentagram made of elder twigs by your door will invoke the blessings and protection of the Dark Goddess, as this tree is sacred to her in her aspect of Crone.

- ✪ An equal-armed cross made of rowan twigs will protect your home from negative magic and is believed to protect against witches and witchcraft!

- ✪ To bring the strength of the oak to a glazed door, choose glass that has an oak-leaf design or an oak-leaf stained-glass panel. (For more about the magic of stained glass see page 55.)

- ✪ An aspen twig placed above the front door will protect against a death in the house and will attract the presence of departed loved ones – this is especially so on the night of Samhain (Halloween), when the veil between the worlds is thinnest.

To seal a door

This very simple ritual should be performed on a daily basis to achieve the best results.

What you need
A stick of incense in your favourite fragrance.

What you do

- ✪ Light the stick of incense and waft it all around the perimeter of the door. This technique is known as smudging.

- ✪ As you smudge the door, repeat the following charm for added security:

> *Doorway to my magical home,*
> *Keep me safe from all who roam,*
> *From those who prowl and those who creep.*
> *Safe and sound this house you keep.*

★ Allow the remaining incense to burn down in a holder near the door and repeat the steps above with each of the external doors to your house.

A potion to invoke the oak

To invoke the strength of the oak tree make up this potion and use it weekly as a magical door wash.

What you need
600 ml/1 pint spring water, a saucepan, 5 oak leaves, 3 acorns, 5 drops oak Bach Flower Remedy, your cauldron or a bowl

What you do
★ Pour the water into the pan and add the oak leaves, acorns and oak Bach Flower Remedy. Simmer gently for about 20 minutes.

★ Transfer the mixture, including the leaves and acorns, into your cauldron or the bowl.

★ Wash all your doors with the potion, as you do so, visualising each one as a mighty drawbridge or a huge and sturdy castle door.

To bring prosperity to your door

This spell will help you to attract prosperity through your door. It uses bay leaves and patchouli, both of which are associated with abundance.

What you need
3 bay leaves, glue, a fine paintbrush, some patchouli essential oil

What you do
★ Hold the three bay leaves between your palms and focus on enjoying a state of prosperity and complete abundance. You can have anything you want, and more.

- Open the main door to your house and carefully glue one bay leaf to the top of it (the part you don't see when the door is closed). Make sure it is glued tight and is flat to the wood so that the door closes properly.
- Glue the second bay leaf on to the side of the door, just below the lock, again making sure that it is glued tight and flat.
- Glue the third leaf inside the letter box, to attract prosperity through the door itself.
- Using the paintbrush and the patchouli oil, paint small invisible currency signs (such as £ or $) in each corner of the door. (Repeat this stage at every full moon to keep the prosperity flowing in.)

Keys

Keys are phallic symbols, and in placing a key in a lock we are unconsciously calling upon the powers of creation and divine union. There are lots of superstitions with regard to keys, the main one being that to wear a key will bring luck and good fortune. This belief is the origin of the modern practice of giving keys as coming-of-age gifts to ensure that the young person in question will have a life filled with blessings. Wearing three keys around your neck is thought to bring health, wealth and happiness, and necklaces of this type are often given as gifts.

Superstition has it that placing a key beneath your pillow will ward off nightmares and protect you during sleep, while putting a cold key down your back will stop a nose bleed. Putting a key in a baby's crib was once thought to guard the baby from faeries, preventing them from putting a changeling in its place. Perhaps this is the reason why rattles and teething toys are often shaped like keys. As keys play a vital role in our security, their main role in the magical home is one of protection.

Key of protection

This spell first appeared in my book *Candleburning Rituals*. It uses a key that does not fit any lock in your house, so you could cast the spell with a friend and exchange a couple of keys. The spell will help to protect your home from burglary, but be sure to back it up with common sense and practical security measures. For the best results, perform the spell on the full moon, when the universal power is at its strongest.

What you need
A white candle, a key that does not fit any lock in your house, your pentacle, a red ribbon

What you do
- ✪ Heat the candle on one side until the wax is soft.
- ✪ Press the key into the wax to make an imprint. Remove the key and place it on your pentacle to charge.
- ✪ Light the candle and repeat the following charm:

> *Those who come with wicked intent*
> *To break my door and steal my rent*
> *Will promptly turn their tail and flee*
> *Due to the magic of my protection key.*
> *So mote it be!*

- ✪ Allow the candle to burn down completely. Thread the key with the red ribbon and hang it above your door to work its magic.

Magic key, come to me ...

We all know how frustrating it is to lose your keys. Although you're sure they have simply been misplaced somewhere near at hand, that knowledge doesn't help when you're hunting under sofas and behind cushions. Next time this happens to you, instead of getting flustered, try this quick spell.
- ✪ Stand still, take three deep breaths and chant the following charm nine times:

> *Magic key, come to me.*

Soon afterwards your keys will turn up, or you will remember where you put them.

Windows

In ancient castles a window was nothing more than a slit in the wall. Perhaps this explains why the modern word 'window' derives from a phrase meaning 'wind's eye'. These old castle windows were sometimes also called 'arrow slits' or 'murder holes', as it was here that the archers would take up their stance, firing arrows down upon the enemy while remaining safe within the castle walls themselves.

Windows give us a glimpse into other people's lives. In winter, when dusk falls early, the sight of homes lit up by lamps urges us to hurry on to the cosy retreat of our own home – especially when the outside world is covered in a blanket of snow.

Magical lore tells us that windows are portals to the spirit world and should never be left undressed. Thus we hang voile, lace, blinds and curtains in our windows. Empty houses are especially vulnerable to invasion by spirits; ghosts are said to take up residence by using clean, shining glass as a doorway. This could be the source of the custom of putting newspaper over the windows when we leave one home to move into another. Another practice is to smear window-cleaning fluid in circles over the panes, again, perhaps in order to prevent spirits from entering the house while it stands empty. Even on modern building sites, once the windows are glazed, large sheets of paper are often put over the glass – although I'm sure the construction workers have no idea of the superstitious origin of this practice!

On New Year's Eve you should open all the windows in your house five minutes before midnight in order to say goodbye to the old year and, as midnight strikes, bid a welcome to the new one. Close the windows again at about five past midnight, allowing the new year time to 'settle in'. Another practice is to open the window of a room in which someone has died, in order to allow the spirit to pass out freely. This tradition is still alive today. A few years ago I spent some time working in a nursing home for the elderly. When a resident died, one of the first things we did was open the window and say goodbye. This custom links in once more with the idea that windows are portals for spirits. You should also open the windows of any room in which there has been an argument between family members, asking the spirits of air to cleanse away the negative energy.

Windows come in all shapes and sizes. Some older houses have

Roman or Gothic arch-shaped windows, while others have perfectly round portholes known as 'moon windows'. In the past, glass could only be made in small pieces, so windows were pieced together like a jigsaw and held together with lead. These mullioned windows have recently undergone a revival. These days you can even buy DIY leading kits, giving you the look in less than a day!

Another old practice that is enjoying a come-back is that of using stained glass. Stained glass can fill your home with the magic of colour and – in an echo of the belief that ghosts can use blank windows as a portal into a home – was once believed to ward off evil spirits. For a real artwork you can you commission a window to your own design from a master craftsman. If you do so, think about incorporating a magical symbol such as a pentagram or a triquetra. Alternatively, you can buy a DIY glass-painting kit and have a go yourself. It is even possible to buy 'stained glass' on a roll. This peels off and sticks to the window, and can be removed easily. This is perfect for those of you who want the look of beautiful stained-glass windows but are living in rented accommodation and so are limited as to what you can do structurally. Another, cheaper, alternative to a stained-glass window is a small stained-glass sun-catcher.

To ward a window

This ritual should be practised daily and at every window.

What you need
Your athame (optional)

What you do
- Using your athame (or your finger if you have no athame or if you want a gentler form of protection), draw a pentagram in the air before each of your windows.

To call the spirits of Air

To invoke the blessings of the Air spirits, the sylphs, choose a beautiful windchime and try this spell.

What you need
A wind chime, your pentacle

What you do

⭐ Place the windchime on your pentacle to charge for three days and nights.

⭐ Hang the windchime in a window that you open daily, as you do so, speaking the following charm:

> *Spirits of Air,*
> *Of grace so rare,*
> *Bring great blessings for me to share!*
> *So mote it be!*

⭐ Gently ring the chimes three times to seal the spell.

Rainbow magic

To fill your home with rainbows, place a faceted crystal in each window of your house. These crystals can be bought in various shapes, including, hearts, flowers, stars and leaves. If it takes you a while to acquire enough of them, just do one window at a time. Place each crystal on your pentacle to charge in the light of the noonday sun before you hang it in your chosen window. As the sun shines through the crystal it will send tiny rainbows dancing all around the room, filling it with colour and sun magic. Be warned, though, if you have a cat he will probably chase these rainbows, so you might want to put breakable items out of the way!

Mirrors

Mirrors are similar to windows but offer a reflection rather than a view. Like windows, they are considered to be portals to other realms, and having two mirrors facing each other is said to invite ghosts into your house. Turning a mirror to face the wall is also believed to open up a magical doorway.

It is very well known that to break a mirror will, it is said, bring seven years of bad luck. This superstition stems from the Roman belief that when you look in a mirror it is your own soul that looks back at you through the glass; to break a mirror was therefore to destroy your soul, which, it was thought, would take seven years to grow back.

Single girls wanting a vision of their future true love or husband are advised to sit before a mirror by candlelight on Halloween, eating an apple and brushing their hair. The vision will appear in the mirror. If you are feeling down, try lighting a candle and telling your troubles to the mirror. You will soon begin to feel better and your reflection may even inspire you with a solution to your problems. It is also said that to give a five-minute pep-talk to your reflection in the mirror each morning will increase your productivity and ensure that you have a great day!

In magic, mirrors are often used to deflect negativity. To this purpose they can be hung, facing outwards, in windows to ward off bad company, unpleasant gossip and nasty neighbours. Some wind chimes have small mirrors attached and so can also be used for this very purpose, especially if you need your magic to be discreet.

On a more practical level, mirrors reflect light and so can make a dark space brighter and a small space seem larger. Having lots of mirrors in the house is traditionally said to attract good luck, five being the perfect number to aim for, while hanging a mirror in the kitchen is thought to bring good food and general abundance to your home. If, like me, you dream of living in the castles of old, invest in four or five stone-framed Gothic arch mirrors and arrange them in a line along a wall or graduated up a staircase to bring a touch of castle-like splendour to your magical home.

Magic mirror spell

In this spell – which turns an ordinary mirror into a magic one – there is a fairytale twist. Use the spell when you have a question that urgently needs an answer.

What you need
A mirror, a piece of chalk, a white candle or tea-light

What you do
⭐ Using the chalk, draw the Asa rune (meaning wisdom) on the back of the mirror. This rune will help to ensure clarity of thought and wise answers to wise questions!

⭐ Darken the room and light the candle or tea-light. Do not use any other illumination. Stand this beyond the mirror so that the flame is not reflected but the glow gently lights your face.

⭐ Stand or sit before the mirror and concentrate on your question, then say the following charm:

> *Mirror, mirror, on the wall,*
> *Hear now this witch's call.*
> *I hold a question in my heart*
> *And beg the wisdom you impart.*
> *The world is not always as it seems,*
> *So reflect the truth within my dreams.*

⭐ Look deep into the reflection of your own eyes and ask the question clearly and out loud.

⭐ Extinguish the candle and take particular note of your dreams for the next seven nights, as that is where you will find your answer. Keeping a dream diary may help you with this.

Transitional Spaces

Transitional spaces are those parts of the home that we simply pass through in order to get from one room to the next. Areas such as porches, hallways and landings are not considered rooms in their own right and as a result they are generally wasted spaces, lacking definition and purpose. However, as most design manuals and home style magazines will tell you, such spaces have great potential. This is especially true when you are creating a magical home.

In the world of witchcraft, transitional areas are considered to be especially powerful, because they are between one thing and another. We have already seen that doors and windows – the most obvious 'in-between' places – have a wealth of superstition and magical practice attached to them, and are considered to be portals to other realms. We can extend this magical way of thinking to include other transitional spaces such as staircases, hallways and landings. And as such spaces are generally without a particular purpose other than that of allowing passage through, it is up to us to define what the space will be. In short, a transitional space can be absolutely anything; you only need to use your imagination.

Porches

Many houses have a small porch around the front or back door. The porch was the forerunner of the conservatory (which we will look at in Chapter 12) and is usually a half-glazed structure of quite small dimensions. It is the perfect place to experiment with stained glass, mirrors and rainbow crystals. As porches are built against the external house wall, they are considered to be an external structure, yet once we are within the porch we are also inside the house, so the porch is an in-between space that can be used to connect with elementals and household spirits.

We can fill the porch with plants, perhaps using it as a greenhouse to grow a few tomatoes or strawberries, or planting a magical herb garden in window boxes and tubs and hanging bunches of herbs to dry from the ceiling. In this way the porch takes on the function of an Elizabethan still-room or a sacred herb pantry, providing us with spells to use in our spell-castings.

The porch can also be used as a place to escape to, functioning as a private retreat or reading room. Although the space is usually small, most porches can house a comfy chair – perhaps a rocking chair or a swinging wicker chair. If this is impossible, you could use a folding chair. Fill your chair with cushions and add a throw, and place an oil-burner and a CD player on the window sill (be sure to take the CD player back into the house when you're not in the porch – don't leave it on display to be stolen!). Now you have a space of your own where you can listen to gentle music, burn soothing oils and read a good novel or study your Wicca books. Sit in the porch and watch the seasons roll by, enjoying the various colours and fragrances that nature offers.

The hallway

The hallway is the first area of your home that people see when entering. As such it should be clean, tidy and sweet-smelling. The door should swing open easily, the decor should be attractive, and the atmosphere should be warm and welcoming. Most importantly for the magical home, the sense of magic and enchantment should sweep over your visitors as soon as they enter.

What guests should not be faced with is a pile of shoes and boots obstructing the door, school bags spilling their contents all over the floor, toys waiting to be stepped on or tripped over, a dirty kitty litter tray (and the smell that goes with it), a bike that ladders stockings or a pushchair that skins unwary shins! The magical home should exude peace, calm and tranquillity, and this begins in the hall.

If your hall is quite dark (as many are) it is important to compensate for this by the clever use of lamps, mirrors and a bright colour scheme.

Creams, mellow yellows and pale blues are all appropriate for hallways, but perhaps the best colour for this area is a beautiful shade of green. There is a practical reason for this. Green is the only colour of the spectrum that our eyes don't need to adapt to; therefore it is very gentle to look at and can create a feeling of instant calm. As green is also the colour of nature, a green hall can make the transition between the garden and the house less jarring to our senses, especially if the decor is enhanced with potted plants and warm lighting.

A mirror hanging in the hall will increase the light and the sense of space, and will immediately deflect any negative energy that comes in from the street. For practical purposes, there should be a mat on which to wipe dirty feet and a place to sit to remove dirty shoes. A decorative coatstand could also be added, and maybe a small chest in which to place shoes, umbrellas and handbags when not in use. Some halls are even large enough to be turned into a reception room, with an open fire and a small sofa.

A hall table is a great place to set up an altar or shrine. This need not be your working altar but could be a magical place dedicated to welcoming people to your home. Burn incense here on a daily basis so that your home always smells fresh. The curling smoke will add a sense of magic. You might also like to keep house plants or freshly cut flowers on your hall table, to add colour and variety. Your hall altar can also reflect the seasons. A bowl of chocolates or fudge provides a welcoming treat for guests – and something to nibble on the drive home, thus giving them a symbol of the warmth and joy of your hospitality to take away with them.

Whatever you decide to use your hall for, remember that this is the first area of your home that people will become acquainted with – even a double glazing salesman will see your hall, if only through the chink in the door! With this in mind, you should place at least one item that speaks of magic and enchantment within this space. This could be a statue of a gargoyle, a picture or woodcarving of a wolf or other power animal, a traditional witches' broom, a water feature or an unusual piece of furniture.

In my hall I have a large CD cabinet fashioned to look like an Egyptian mummy sarcophagus. It stands facing the front door and is the first thing that people see. Not only is it something of a talking point, but it acts as a magical guardian, protecting my house. One look at it and people know they are in a different kind of home – they may not be able to put their finger on it, but they can feel the magic, and on some level they just know that they have entered a witch's house!

The staircase

As an area that is in-between floors, the staircase is yet another portal. This could be the reason that ghostly footsteps are often heard walking up and down stairs, and spirits are sometimes seen walking a staircase that no longer exists, often disappearing through the roof or the floor. Although a small and relatively narrow space, a staircase can be used most effectively as an art gallery. Here you can arrange your favourite family photographs in beautiful frames as testimony to your heritage and family tree. Or you can hang a collection of needlepoint projects you have completed or pictures you have painted.

To make the staircase in keeping with your magical home, think about introducing a magical theme – art work by fantasy artists such as Briar, Jack Shalatain or Linda Garland can help to turn an ordinary staircase into a truly sacred space. Posters of dragons, unicorns, faeries and other fantasy creatures can be used too. Alternatively, you can decorate on a particular theme, such as Gothic, using images of wolves and vampires, and wall plaques fashioned to look like gargoyles and bats – they're all out there just waiting to be discovered! If you favour a medieval staircase, you can hang tapestries, torch-style candle sconces, arched mirrors and heavy door-curtains.

Don't forget the space under the stairs. If this area is open-plan, you could use it as a PC station and set up your computer desk and chair here. On the other hand, you could arrange several wine racks in it, turning it into something of a wine cellar. If the space is enclosed, it can be used as storage space for the hoover and ironing board, the kids toys, or your riding gear or sports equipment. If the space is large, you could put in some good lighting and set up your sewing machine in it, creating a small sewing room. Use your imagination and turn these neglected areas into something special that works for you.

Landings

If your home has a large landing, this, again, is space that can be put to good use. If there is a window, you could put in a desk and chair and turn it into a study or home office, or install a second PC for the kids. Alternatively, line the walls with bookcases or shelves and use the landing space as a library for all your books, videos, CDs and DVDs. Think about the space you have and what potential is currently being ignored.

Witch bottle spell

A witch bottle is a traditional tool of protection. Some are filled with sharp objects such as pins, needles, and bits of broken glass and mirror – this is a banishing bottle. Others are filled with bits of fabric and thread, and are used to tangle up any negative energies that come your way. Others still are filled with sand or grain, which not only deflects negativity but also deters evil spirits. Tradition has it that should a malevolent spirit enter the house, it will not be able to stay until it has counted every grain of sand in the bottle. You can make as many witch bottles as you like and dot them around your home.

What you need
An attractive bottle or jar with a tightly fitting lid, sand or grains in a variety of shades and colours (different coloured bath salts work well and look attractive too)

What you do
- ✪ Make sure your bottle is clean and dry, and then begin to fill it with the salts, layering the various colours and tapping the bottle occasionally to make they lie flat.
- ✪ Once your bottle is full, put the lid on tightly, hold it in your hands and say:

  Witch bottle, witch bottle, hear the words I say:
  Protect from negativity; keep hurt and harm away.

- ✪ Place the witch bottle in a transitional space in your house, such as the hallway, porch or staircase, to protect and guard the magical portals within your home.

Spell of welcome

Use this spell to empower a bowl of sweets or chocolates with a magical welcome for your guests. Once offered a treat from the bowl, friends and family will love coming to your home, although they may not know exactly why. Indeed, your home may well become the designated meeting place in your circle!

What you need
A pretty bowl, some brightly wrapped chocolates or sweets, a packet of incense sticks in your favourite fragrance and a suitable holder

What you do

✪ Put the sweets or chocolates in the bowl, hold your hands over them and speak the following charm:

> *These treats so sweet are here to share*
> *With friends and loved ones for whom I care.*
> *Let them feel and know my love,*
> *And feel the magic of the powers above.*
> *So mote it be!*

✪ Hold the packet of incense sticks between your palms and say:

> *Welcome friends and loved ones dear;*
> *Protect and guard them while they're here.*
> *When once they leave this calm abode,*
> *Guide them on their chosen road.*
> *Until once more they choose to call,*
> *Their laughter echoes within these walls.*
> *So mote it be!*

✪ Whenever you have guests, offer them one of your magically charged treats and light the incense. Remember to repeat the spell every time you buy new incense sticks or goodies.

Protection of the ghost chair

This spell is a great way to protect your home at any time when you are away.

What you need

A chair – or chairs if there is more than one entrance to your house (dining chairs will do)

What you do

⭐ Place the chair so that it faces the front door to your house. It is said that this will invite a friendly ghost (maybe an ancestor) to watch over your home while you are away. If you have another external door, place a chair facing that too.

⭐ Silently request the chairs and their ghostly occupants to guard and protect your home in your absence. When you return home, don't forget to thank the friendly spirits before you put the chairs back in their correct place.

Correspondences for the hallway and transitional spaces

Oils and incenses	Crystals	Angels	Elementals	Power animals
Blackberry	Clear quartz	Michael	Salamander	Dragon
Apple	Aventurine			Wolf
Patchouli	Hematite			Peacock
Sage	Obsidian			Badger
Basil				
Orange				
Rosemary				

The Magical Lounge

As the lounge is central to family life, it should have an atmosphere of peace and calm. Key words for this room include cosy, quiet, tranquil and safe.

Too often, the main function of the lounge is to house the TV, in front of which we sit slumped, never saying a dozen words to one another all evening. Needless to say, this is not the best way to build a magical home; indeed, it can create a stale and even hostile atmosphere. This is not to say that you should not watch television, but you should moderate your viewing. TV can be entertaining and educational – but it is also addictive. Don't fall into the trap of staring at the screen just for the sake of it. You have better things to do with your life.

A great way to stop yourself watching too much TV is to shut the television away. Buy a TV cabinet with doors so that you can put temptation out of view. If you have one of those super-wide-screen, surround-sound, does-everything-but-the-washing-up entertainment systems, hide it away by placing a pretty folding screen in front of it.

Screens

Screens have made a welcome come-back in the last few years and are no longer the sole property of the period home's Victorian parlour. Carved from wood, wrought in iron or woven from wicker, screens can be used for a variety of purposes within the magical home. If you have a PC or home office set up in the corner of your lounge, an attractive screen can conceal your work area. Screens can also be used to hide your magical altar from visitors or to section off a corner of the room to create a quiet space for contemplation, meditation and so on. Some modern screens have a dual purpose, being designed to accommodate your CD collection or your family photos.

My own lounge has a three-fold screen made out of pewter-effect wrought iron. It is of a branch, leaf and berry design, and has glass cups that hold tea-lights. When all the tea-lights are lit they throw shadows of branches and leaves across the room, giving it a Sleepy Hollow woodland effect. Such screens are becoming very popular, so have a look in your local shopping arcade or department store if you'd like to include one in your own magical home. Screens are also relatively easy to make, so if you enjoy DIY you could come up with an individual design all of your own.

Furnishing the lounge

Other furnishings in the lounge should be warm and comfortable, and include enough seating space to accommodate all members of the family. Lots of cushions are essential to encourage cosy evenings in, and it's a good idea to include a variety of throws if you have children or pets, as they can be changed in an instant and are easily cleaned. This can prevent a lot of stress and prevent you from being labelled a nag! A bowl of fruit on a coffee table will encourage healthy nibbling, as can bowls of nuts dotted around the room. This casual offer of food actually harks back to an ancient rite of hospitality.

To increase the feeling of magic in the lounge, pay attention to how you accessorise. Oil and incense burners are a must for the lounge of a magical house. They come in a wide variety of shapes and styles, so you should be able to find something you like. If your interest in magic is well known, you could have a collection of witch figures on the mantelpiece, or wizards on the hearth. If you need to be more discreet, there is a variety of ways to bring in a magical touch without making it obvious to anyone but you. You could, for instance, decorate in shades of deep purple, plum and aubergine, and add a touch of gold to create a magical back-drop. Dark blues and silver will create a similar magical effect. Velvet curtains embroidered with silver stars, and soft furnishings brocaded with a fleur de lys design will both help to create the enchanted look you're aiming for – both stars and fleur de lys are magical symbols. Figures and pictures of animals associated with witchcraft and paganism (see my book *Magical Beasts* for more information on this subject) can also be introduced. Deer, stags, owls, cats and wolves are all good for this purpose.

A friend of mine recently married a *bona fide* magical sceptic and has had to take his needs into account when furnishing their home. She has chosen a neutral colour scheme, opting for natural materials such as wood, cotton, leather and seagrass. To an outsider, her house is simply a series of lovely rooms that have been well put together, but to those in the know the signs of magic are there. A basket of fir cones stands amid candles on the hearth. A fairy cottage and a pixie sit on the mantelpiece next to a vase depicting a salamander. A couple of hedgehog statues are displayed by the TV. Tea-lights are contained in leaf-style holders and fitted into wooden apples. In the kitchen, a pagan cookbook sits open on a bookstand, and a wicker egg-holder hangs from a beam. If you look closely at the baker's rack that hangs from the ceiling, you will find a tiny witch flying her broomstick amid the pans and utensils. Outside, a broomstick stands by the back door and a statue of a rabbit sits on a stone wall, looking out across the fields. So you see, there are ways and means of creating a magical home without having witchcraft screaming from every corner.

Furniture folklore

A wealth of superstition has grown up around home furniture. Rounded furniture is considered to be the most magical, as it echoes the shape of the moon. Round tables are especially powerful, because they encourage equality and forge a magical link with the legend of King Arthur and his Knights of the Round Table. The number 13 being generally considered of ill omen, it is believed by some to be unlucky to have 13 guests around a dinner table. In witchcraft, however, 13 (the number of lunations in the solar year) is a sacred number, so in the magical home a gathering of 13 would be truly blessed.

A rocking chair that rocks by itself is a sign that an ancestor is visiting in order to watch over you. Give them a word of welcome to your home and thank them for their protection. If a dining chair falls over as someone stands, it is an indication that that person has deceived you in some way, while a guest who returns their chair to its rightful place is unlikely to visit your home again. Take care how you place your chairs, as putting them opposite one another will breed confrontation and negativity. Placing them at right-angles, however, will encourage love and trust, and so foster a harmonious atmosphere.

In the past, most homes had a grandfather clock in the hall. If this clock struck 13, it was believed to be a warning of misfortune the following day. On the other hand, a wish made at the 12th stroke of midnight on New Year's Eve is said to be certain to come true – so wish well and wisely!

And finally, a couple of candle superstitions ... If a burning candle falls over, it is said to be a sign of bad luck – not surprisingly, as a fallen candle could set the whole house on fire! A candle flame that gutters when there is no draught is an indication that a spirit has walked by.

Magic carpets

Carpets and rugs do more than just add a sense of warmth to a room; they can also bring an air of magic and enchantment. The most magical rugs are round, oval or semi-circular in shape, representing the full moon, the cosmic egg and the half-moon respectively. A special round rug can be used in magic to define the space of the magic circle. Surrounded by candles in a darkened room, this is a magic carpet indeed! Rectangular rugs can be used to create a magical path – the common-all-garden hall runner is a classic example of this, forming a pathway into the heart of the home.

To keep rugs fresh and sweet-smelling, sprinkle them with lavender water. This practice harks back to medieval times, when floors were strewn with rushes, petals and dried herbs.

Remember, too, that rugs are not just for the floor, but can be hung on walls or over doors as door curtains to bring a touch of medieval elegance to your home. Some New Age stores sell rugs with magical designs, such as pentagrams, suns, moons, stars and Green Men woven into them. Rugs with Celtic knotwork designs are also available. Any of these would be a perfect addition to the magical home.

To make a perfect peace potion

This potion is great for maintaining a calm and peaceful atmosphere within your home. It should be sprayed around the house every day, while an extra blast after a family argument will help to dispel any lingering negativity and restore tranquillity.

What you need
600 ml (1 pint) spring water (if you can obtain it from a local well or spring, so much the better; otherwise, use the bottled variety), 3 drops lemon balm essential oil, 3 drops apple essential oil, 3 drops melon essential oil, a spritzer bottle, a label

What you do
- To the spring water add the lemon balm oil (for purification), apple oil (for love, peace and happiness) and melon oil (for healing).
- Transfer the potion into the spritzer bottle and label it 'Perfect Peace Potion'. Shake the bottle well.
- Hold the bottle between your palms and say:

  I empower this potion with the gift of peace.
  So mote it be!

  Your potion is now ready for use.

A gratitude box

Sometimes it can be difficult to tell a person how much we love and appreciate them. This is especially true where children and teenagers are concerned – adults are usually quick to jump on kids when they do something wrong, but often forget to praise them when they actually do something right! Keeping a gratitude box will help to prevent any family member feeling invisible or taken for granted. If you want to involve your children in making one, make them responsible for decorating it in some way.

What you need

A box or container of some sort, material to decorate the box (optional),
a little rose water, a pad and pencil

What you do

- ☆ If you want to, decorate your box in any way you choose (or invite your children to do so).
- ☆ Sprinkle the box with the rose water to infuse it with love. This is now your family's gratitude box. Place it in the lounge and put a pad and pencil next to it.
- ☆ Now your gratitude box is ready to be used. The idea is that each week every member of the family writes a 'thank you' or a 'well done' to each of the other family members (so that no-one gets left out) and places it in the box. These need not be for huge things. For example, they might include a thanks to mum for cooking a great meal, or to dad for fixing the family car (or vice versa in some homes), a well done to a child for getting good marks in a spelling test, or a word of acknowledgement to a teenager who has made more effort to revise for an exam or clean their room. Once a week, while all the family members are present – perhaps around the Sunday lunch table – open the box and read out what has been written. This routine will help to increase family bonding and will enable everyone to hear what we all need to every once in a while: 'I love you and appreciate all that you do.'

Hearth magic

Since time immemorial, families have gathered around the hearth. The earliest homes were round structures with a central hearth. Here tribespeople would gather around the fire and tell stories to one another as a way of preserving their history, educating the younger generation and, of course, entertaining themselves. In medieval times it was before the roaring fire of the Great Hall that minstrels, jongleurs and troubadours strummed their lutes and sang their romantic tales.

In the past, the hearth was where meals were cooked, scrying and divinations performed, healing potions brewed, stories told, and heat and warmth enjoyed by the family gathered around the banked-up fire – where they would also sleep. Sacred to Goddesses such as Hestia and Vesta (see pages 33–4) it was thus associated with women's mysteries. These days, the lounge is generally the place that contains the domestic hearth, even if it is in the form of a gas fire. However, many of the activities traditionally belonging to it have been divided up and reallocated to various rooms in the home. We sleep in centrally heated bedrooms, for instance, and cook in the kitchen with modern stoves and microwave ovens. The hearth is no longer central to our existence, and much of its magic has escaped us.

Perhaps the only time we truly feel the magic of the sacred fire is on the 5th of November, when families gather around the bonfire in commemoration of the Gunpowder Plot. There are fireworks, of course, and a feast of jacket potatoes, parkin, chestnuts and hot stews is enjoyed. Here in Britain the tradition of celebrating Halloween has all but died out, the occasion marked only by some fairly low-key dressing-up and trick-or-treating by children. In the past, however, All Hallows Eve was a great fire festival enjoyed by people of all ages. Perhaps we could learn something from our American cousins, who celebrate Halloween with great enthusiasm, building bonfires, organising street parties, and decorating their homes with scarecrows, pumpkins, witches, black cats, vampires and bats.

If we want to bring the magic back into our homes, one way or another we must reconnect with the hearth. Of course, it can be difficult to find the sacred fire as we pop a box into the microwave, but this does not mean we cannot link the threads of past and present; it simply means that our connection will be different from that of our ancestors. In the modern magical home we have to learn how to merge the ancient skills of hearth magic with the conveniences of modern living. We need to begin to regard the hearth as the heart of the magical home and the lounge as a sacred space that will nurture our family and relationships if only we let it.

Putting the heart back into the hearth

Most lounges have a hearth of some kind, with a mantelpiece above. If all you have is a gas fire set on the wall, then create a fireplace by fixing up a shelf as a mantlepiece and laying down a row of flat stones or pieces of marble as a hearth. If you live by the sea, a plank of driftwood could create an unusual hearth and will bring the natural powers of both the woodland and the ocean to your home.

Once you have your hearth, clean it with a solution of warm water to which three tablespoonfuls of rose water have been added. The rose is the flower of love, so when you clean with a rose water mixture, you are putting your love back into your home. Take your time and concentrate on the magical powers of the hearth as you carry out your task. Call on Vesta to help you (see page 34) and clean slowly and methodically, knowing that your work is an act of reverence.

Next pour ten drops of cedarwood essential oil onto a clean pad of cotton wool. Rub the oil into the wood, bricks and tiles of the hearth and mantlepiece using slow circular motions. Cedarwood oil gives off a wonderful woody fragrance that will linger around your hearth for days. Once again, as you work concentrate on the magical powers of the hearth.

Finally, find a representation of a heart – for example a heart-shaped tea-light-holder or a small cushion – and place it on the hearth. This is a symbolic way of putting the heart back into your home and will help you to begin making your lounge magical. But there is still much to do.

Rekindle the living flame

Living flames are vital to the magical home. Whether they are in the form of an open log or coal fire, a modern 'living flame' gas fire, or a collection of candles doesn't really matter, but it is essential that fire is present in some form. If you are already involved in magic or witchcraft, you will probably have a collection of candles and tea-lights, as these are staples of the witch's store cupboard. If you cannot have a real fire in your hearth, rekindle the hearth flame by placing a small collection of candles, candlesticks, lanterns and so on on your hearth, and lighting them regularly. If your hearth is wide enough, you could use floating candles in a bowl. This will bind the usually opposing powers of fire and water and will create a truly sacred flame.

Prayer to Vesta

Spending a few moments each day communing with Vesta will bring about an almost immediate change in your relationship with your home. You will find that you feel much more connected with it and may be inspired to make a few home improvements. Vesta can help you to attune with our own inner magic and with the deeper magic of women's mysteries. She will instil a sense of calm and control – no more running around like a headless chicken when confronted with a minor domestic crisis – and can teach you how to shrug your shoulders and laugh at yourself rather than becoming consumed with feelings of inadequacy because you put up pictures using carpet tacks and a toffee hammer ... or maybe that's just me! Vesta's energies will also be felt by other family members, inducing a sense of companionship, peace and family bonding. The best time to perform this little prayer is in the evening when the house is quiet.

✪ Sit comfortably before the hearth and invoke the living flame by lighting your hearth candles or turning on the gas fire.

✪ Once the flames have taken form and shape, say the following prayer:

> *Goddess Vesta, hear this plea:*
> *Let women's magic flow from me.*
> *Shine your blessings on this home;*
> *Bond my family – let none roam.*
> *Teach me the skills and pride of the true housewife;*
> *Let joy and enchantment fill my life.*
> *Fill this house with love and calm;*
> *Keep those within safe from harm.*
> *When things go wrong, still let me see*
> *The domestic Goddess I aim to be!*
> *I ask this boon, so shall it be!*
> *Goddess Vesta, blessed be!*

✪ Repeat this prayer each evening for the best ongoing results.

Spell to invoke the protection of the salamander

As the elementals of fire, salamanders should be represented at your hearth in some way – a small figure of a dragon or lizard is appropriate. Repeating this spell every full moon will protect your home from accidental fire, lightning strikes and so on.

What you need
A representation of a salamander

What you do
✪ Hold your hands, palms down, over your salamander representation and invoke its protection by saying the following charm three times:

Salamander, hear my desire:
Protect my home from all destructive fire.

Candle time

Our lives are often so hectic that we rarely take the time to sit and wind down at the end of a busy day. However, some quiet time is essential if we are to sleep well and enjoy a restful night – especially for children and teenagers. Try making candle time part of your daily routine. It will benefit all the family, improving sleeping patterns and possibly even opening up new lines of communication.

At around 8pm turn the TV off and put on some quiet soothing music, such as Enya. Then light candles and place them around the lounge. Turn off all other lights and burn a relaxing incense or oil such as lavender. Have something special to nibble on and enjoy a nice drink – a small glass of wine could be just the thing to tempt teenagers to take part, while warm milky drinks have a sedative effect, especially on small children. Another natural way to relax is to install an aquarium and watch the fish gliding in and out of the plants. This is also a great way to calm babies and toddlers.

Because there are no distractions, you may find that your children open up to you more than usual, telling you about their day and any problems they may have, while the romantic atmosphere of candlelight and soft music may prompt your partner to make alternative suggestions for relaxation!

Try having candle time for a week or so and see how it goes. It may be a battle at first, but eventually your family will begin to feel the benefits and may even start to look forward to these quieter evenings.

Correspondences for the lounge

Oils and incenses	Crystals	Angels	Elementals	Power animals
Calendula	Clear quartz	Gabriel	Gnome	Wolf
Apple	Rose quartz	Raphael	Sylph	Badger
Basil	Citrine		Salamander	
Bergamot	Amethyst			
Sweetpea				
Melon				
Lemon balm				
Lilac				
Bluebell				
Jasmine				
Lily of the valley				

THE MAGICAL LOUNGE

The Hedge Witch's Kitchen

K itchen witching is a very important part of the Craft. It is in the kitchen that herbs are dried and empowered to a particular magical purpose, incenses are blended, potions and draughts are concocted, and, of course, nutritious meals are prepared and cooked for the family. Often the kitchen becomes something of a gathering place for family and friends, particularly if the room is large enough to house a table and chairs.

In the past, the kitchen was the most important room in the house, particularly in winter, when it was often the only room with a source of heat. Because of this, kitchens were usually quite large, with space for seating areas as well as a dining table and chairs. Imagine for a moment the traditional farmhouse kitchen. There is a warm glow from the Aga, rugs brighten up the flagstone floor, deep chairs flank the fireside, and a cat is curled up on the window seat. The land around may be barren and bare, but the farmhouse table is laden with loaves, pies, joints of meat and vegetables of all kinds. This is a scene of homely comfort and abundance.

Compare this vision with one of a modern kitchen. Often 'streamlined' to tiny proportions, and shining with silver and chrome or gleaming snowy white, today's kitchens can be clinical in appearance and cold in atmosphere. It is as if the life has been sucked out of them. They are devoid of a fireplace, soft furnishings and comfortable places to sit, while most of the food preparation that goes on in them consists of taking a box out of the freezer and popping it in the microwave.

Now, I'm not saying that a woman's place is in the kitchen chained to the stove. Nor am I asking you to throw out the microwave and stop buying convenience foods – in fact, convenience foods can be a life-saver, especially if, like me, you have minimal culinary skills. What I am saying is that we need to reconnect with the sacred aspects of the kitchen, becoming far more aware of what we actually do in this part of the house. We need to bring magic back into our neglected kitchens and see them for what they truly are: the lynch pin of the covenstead.

The covenstead

The covenstead is the place where witches make magic. For a coven of witches working together, the covenstead is wherever their regular meeting place is. To the solitary witch, however, the covenstead is her own home.

While many spells and formal rituals are performed at the altar, other impromptu spells may be cast in the kitchen. Just as the hearth is the symbolic heart of the family home, so the kitchen is the backbone of the covenstead and the stage for the hedge witch's power. It is thus vital to the magical home that we put the enchantment back into the kitchen, acknowledging it as the realm of the wise woman.

To do this you do not need to be a cordon bleu chef or a culinary whizz kid. There is as much magic in making a soothing cup of tea for a distressed friend as there is in whipping up dinner for eight. The trick is to see the magic in all things, and through that vision to reconnect with the ancient powers of the wise woman that lie within all of us. This chapter will help you to do just that, giving you practical ways to turn your vision around and regard your kitchen as a sacred place of magic and the centre of your covenstead.

Hedge witching

Hedge witches are particularly concerned with traditional green arts, such as making herbal potions and spells. They are often solitaries; in other words, they work alone rather than as part of a coven. Historically, a hedge witch was often the village wise woman (or wise man), to whom people would come for cures and advice. It stands to reason, therefore, that the kitchen is the particular realm of the hedge witch. Almost all witches, however, whether or not they would define themselves as a hedge witch, will make use of hedge magic in many of their spells and rituals.

Setting the scene for magic

The kitchen of the magical home should be, first and foremost, as fresh and clean and nicely decorated as you can make it. All utensils and gadgets should be put away neatly unless they are in regular use. If you can, steer clear of plastic and man-made storage; opt instead for wood, wicker, cotton and so on – a set of wicker baskets can provide a good storage solution, while bringing a natural look to your kitchen. Other ideas for storage are chests and trunks, airing racks, and baker's racks, and hampers. If you have a wood or stone floor, consider leaving it in its natural state. If this is not possible, try to use floor coverings that give as natural a feel as possible. Once your kitchen is sparkling clean and all modern gadgets are neatly tucked away out of sight, you have a blank canvas on which to work a little magic ...

The kitchen altar

The simplest way to bring magic to your kitchen is to set up a little altar. This could be on a dresser, shelf or window sill, or on top of the fridge-freezer. By creating a small space dedicated to magic in your kitchen, you are inviting the enchantment back into this room. A candle should be central to your altar. This should be lit regularly – whenever you go into the kitchen to create a potion or cook a meal for the family – so a tea-light in a suitable holder is the most practical. Some witches, however, prefer to use a beeswax candle, which will also fill with room with its natural honeyed fragrance.

Place on your altar some form of goddess figure to represent the idea that all food is from the earth and therefore from the Great Goddess. Figures of Demeter, Gaia, Sabd or even a small faerie are all appropriate. If you don't mind people knowing of your interest in the Craft, a kitchen altar is a great place to put a statue of a stereotypical witch, complete with black pointed hat, cauldron, broom and familiar. These can be bought very cheaply around Halloween, so keep a look out. You could take this idea further by buying witches flying on broomsticks to hang from the ceiling. Smaller versions can be hung from cupboard doors and in windows. I have one of these witches hanging from the rear view mirror of my car, and I have to say it does attract a certain amount of attention!

Add to your altar a small jar of salt (to represent abundance and prosperity) and an oil-burner. Try to burn seasonal fragrances – for example, blossom scents in spring; fruit and flowers in summer; apples and berries in autumn; and pine, cinnamon and ginger in winter. This will help you to attune with the seasons and the natural world around you. Finally, your kitchen altar should hold some representation of cooking – miniature food and utensils designed for a doll's house are perfect. Use your imagination, hunt for bargains if you're short of cash and ask your household spirits to help you create an enchanting kitchen altar.

Magical tools of the kitchen witch

In addition to the standard witch's tools described on pages II–I2, there are several items that no serious kitchen witch would be without ...

Wooden spoon

The wooden spoon is the wand incognito! It can be used, in exactly the same way as a wand, to direct energy into the food being prepared or cooked. Always stir deosil (clockwise), thus following the path of the sun and bringing blessings and good health to the food and those who partake of it. Use the wooden spoon to draw a pentagram in foods as you stir, or over the foods you are preparing. This, again, will bless the food and add to its magic.

Cookbook stand

A cookbook stand is not only practical but magical as well. Bookstands have been used for centuries to hold sacred books – thus creating an altar of knowledge. If you want to see how magical a simple bookstand can be, take a look in any traditional church – or watch an episode of *Charmed*. Try to obtain a table-top one that is adjustable so that you can alter the slope of the book. Also make sure the bookstand will hold open pages in some way. My own bookstand is made of iron and has silver chains with weighted ball bearings on the end to secure the pages of the book. Introducing a bookstand is a great way to transform the kitchen instantly into a place of magic. Try it for yourself. Place a witch's cookbook or your copy of *How to Create a Magical Home* on it and see how witchy your kitchen suddenly becomes! You may even be inspired to buy a floor-standing bookstand for your altar room to keep your Book of Shadows (or witch's book of spells) on.

Chopping board

You can buy magical chopping boards with a pentagram design in occult shops. They act in the same way that a pentacle would, magically charging the food as you prepare it. They are almost essential when working with herbs. You can make your own by painting a large pentagram on a round chopping board using a non-toxic food-safe paint – most craft stores will be able to advise you on this. Once the paint has dried, wash the board in warm salt water to cleanse it. Use it when preparing food as well as in your magical herbal workings.

Mortar and pestle

Mortar and pestle are staples of the kitchen witch – an absolute must if you wish to work with herbs and make your own scattering powders and incenses. By grinding the ingredients by hand rather than using a food processor, you can focus on your magical intent, pouring your power into the herbs and spices as you work. You should grind deosil (clockwise) for most spells – unless you are preparing a banishing mixture, in which case grind widdershins (anti-clockwise). A collection of mortars and pestles arranged on a shelf would really bring the magic of the wise woman to your kitchen!

Trivets

Cast-iron trivets with three legs are a symbol of the Great Goddess as provider of abundance. They are often decorated with fruits, flowers, stars and sheaves of corn – all symbols of plenty. They can magically attract prosperity to your home as well as protecting surfaces and worktops from hot pans.

Cauldron

Every witch's kitchen has a cauldron, whether this be a traditional cast-iron one or one of its modern descendants – the saucepan and the casserole dish. The latter is fine if you prefer to keep your interest in magic and witchcraft to yourself, but do try to get the largest one you can, preferably in a dark colour such as blue or black.

For those of you who are more adventurous, genuine Wiccan cauldrons can be bought in a variety of sizes, so you should be able to find one to suit your budget. And nothing looks more magical than a

THE HEDGE WITCH'S KITCHEN

cast-iron three-legged cauldron standing waiting on the stove. Even if for practical purposes you prefer to work with saucepans (and many modern witches do) tiny cauldrons designed to hold tea-lights are available in the shops around Halloween and would look great on a kitchen altar or dotted around the room.

According to tradition, your cauldron should always be placed ready on the stove, not put away in a cupboard. This is the case whether you use a proper Wiccan cauldron, or a modern saucepan or casserole dish. Your cauldron should also always be washed by hand and not put through the dish-washer. As long as your cauldron is scrupulously clean, you can use it to heat food such as soups, stews and milk puddings, thus automatically instilling them with magic. After all, foods and drinks are themselves magical potions when we regard them as such and honour their powers.

Ladle

Just as the wooden spoon is the wand incognito, so the ladle is a miniature cauldron. Its deep round belly represents the fertility of the goddess and of all life. Use it to dispense seasonal punches from the main cauldron or to pour magical potions into your sacred chalice.

The seasonal kitchen

No other room in the house reflects the turning wheel of the seasons quite as clearly as the kitchen. The foods we prepare and eat change according to the season – we enjoy crisp salads and ice creams in summer, and hot soups and stews in winter. The seasonal fragrances of our cooking and magical workings fill the kitchen, be they berry pies baking in the oven in autumn or blossom potions simmering in spring. In modern Western society we are lucky enough to be able to enjoy a wide range of out-of-season foods; try not to lose sight of what is actually in season, however. You might like to make a special meal once a week using only foods that are seasonally available. This will help you to attune with the natural energies around you and will improve your skills and power as a kitchen witch.

Another way to deepen your connection with the passing year is to add a single seasonal item to the kitchen altar; alternatively, you can decorate the entire kitchen with seasonal images and objects, thus ensuring that you are constantly reminded of womanly wisdom, and of the fact that the earth and ourselves are inextricably linked. The following are some suggestions that you might like to use for seasonal decorations; if, however, you prefer to come up with your own ideas, that's fine too.

Spring

In spring, bring in vases of the first flowers. Daffodils and tulips will brighten up even the drabbest kitchen, while jugs of blossoms suggest an air of the countryside cottage, no matter where you live. Eggs in any form are great spring decorations. Chocolate, hard-boiled, hand-painted, wooden and even glass or wicker eggs can be placed in baskets or hung from cupboard doors on pretty ribbons. Add a few figures of rabbits, chicks, hares and lambs, and burn a spring blossom oil in your oil-burner, and your kitchen will vibrate with the magical energies of spring.

Summer

Summer calls for more flowers – foxgloves and roses are great for bringing the scent of summer indoors. As we enjoy the new strength of the sun and the long hot days, add candle-holders in sun shapes. Bright yellow or gold tablecloths and napkins also speak of the summer sunshine, and a mobile of bees around a honey pot or hive will remind you that summer is a time of industry for some of our wildlife.

Autumn

Autumn is, of course, the season of the turning leaves, so make use of candle-holders, fabrics and crockery with leaf designs. Hang wreaths of artificial apples, pears, pine cones and acorns around the kitchen. Sheaves of corn, poppies, corn dollies and baskets of berries will all help to bring this season of transformation into your kitchen. Burn apple and blackberry incense as you bake a pie of these same fruits, and remember that the witches' most important sabbat (or festival), Samhain, falls within this season (on 31 October), so honour it by investing in a cauldron, making a pumpkin lantern and hanging up witch decorations. This is also a good time to buy a decorative broom to hang in your kitchen.

Winter

Come the winter, it is a good idea to warm up the home with scents of ginger, clove and cinnamon, while pine is a great fragrance for bringing in the fresh tang of Yuletide. Bunches of mistletoe can be hung from the ceiling to add a feeling of Druid magic. Decorations could include five-pointed stars, bells, reindeer, stags, a small Yuletide tree and maybe a garland made of holly, ivy, nuts and cones.

If the area of seasonal magic interests you, you might like to read my book *The Witch's Almanac*, which contains lots of spells, rituals, exercises and ideas for seasonal living.

Victorian wisdom

For most of us, the daily chores of running a home can be a bit of a bind, to say the least. Perhaps we should take a tip from the Victorian ladies and create a household routine. This strategy harks back to the teachings of Hestia and Vesta, by which little and often is the key to magical housework.

You could, for example, put the washing in on Monday, do the ironing on Tuesday, go shopping on Wednesday (so avoiding the weekend crowds), do general cleaning on Thursday ... and so on. I must stress that this is just an example, and I realise that many of your lives will involve such responsibilities as a full-time job, shift work, children (a child being a full-time job in its own right), elderly relatives and so on. Only you know what demands you have and how you can best schedule the household chores that need to be done. However, by creating a routine for yourself, you will find that after a while things begin to run like clockwork, leaving you more time for yourself and your magic.

Wort cunning

Wort cunning is the ancient art of magical herbalism and is an important part of the hedge witch's work. It is in the kitchen that the skills of wort cunning take centre stage, and even the most modern kitchen usually houses a spice rack filled with jars of dried herbs and spices. A witch's kitchen is generally full of jars of powders and potions, and even racks of test tubes, all waiting to be put to a magical use.

If herbalism interests you, begin collecting empty jars. Ask friends and relatives for old coffee jars, jam jars, peanut butter jars and so on. Soak off the old labels and make sure you give the jars a good clean. You can then fill them with dried herbs, which will be the basis for any incenses or scattering powders you make. You will also need:

- ✪ More jars to keep your incense blends and potions in
- ✪ Charcoal blocks to burn incenses on
- ✪ Test tubes and a test-tube rack for the blending and storing of some powders
- ✪ A mortar and pestle
- ✪ Sticky labels to identify your herbs, powders and blends
- ✪ A selection of essential oils and Bach Flower Remedies – which can be bought gradually as needed, or invested in one or two at a time, as and when you can afford them
- ✪ A good book on magical herbalism, such as *A Wiccan Herbal* by Marie Rodway
- ✪ A Book of Shadows (or magical journal) in which to record all your favourite potions, blends and recipes – a simple notebook will do

✪ A chest or special cupboard to keep all your wort cunning equipment in

I keep all my herbs and equipment in my Egyptian mummy cabinet. It is cool and dark, which is essential if you don't want your herbs, oils and potions to spoil, and is a very magical kind of storage space! You could also keep your herbal equipment on a set of shelves along the kitchen wall, or in a dresser or a carved wooden chest. Place your book of magical herbalism on your bookstand so that you always know where to find it and have it easily to hand when you are working.

Don't feel that you have to buy all your wort cunning equipment at once. A witch's herbal cabinet is usually built up over a period of time, so buy what you need for each spell as you go along, and you will eventually have a store cupboard full of magical herbs and equipment.

The following are a couple of simple herbal spells to get you started on this hedge witch's art ...

Kitchen witch incense

This incense is perfect for burning on a charcoal block at your kitchen altar and will fill the house with the fine fragrance of the hedge witch's herbal magic.

What you need
1 clove, 1 tsp ground cinnamon, 1 tsp ground ginger, 2 tsp dried mugwort, 1 tsp dried basil, a mortar and pestle, 2 drops cedarwood essential oil, 2 drops oak moss essential oil, a censer (available from New Age and some Indian goods shops), a clean jar, a label

What you do
✪ Into the mortar place the clove, cinnamon, ginger, mugwort and basil. Grind all the herbs together, using the pestle in a deosil (clockwise) direction. As you do so, focus strongly on the magic of the wise woman and silently call on the powers of the ancestral witches of your bloodline – don't worry if you don't know of any; there's bound to be at least one witch in your ancestry!

- ✪ Add the cedarwood and oak moss essential oils, imagining the incense taking on the powers of the hedge witch and the green earth as you do so. Continue to mix well with the pestle.
- ✪ Hold your palms over the incense and imagine a strong white light going from your hands into the mixture.
- ✪ Burn three pinches of the incense on your kitchen altar in the censer right away. Transfer the rest of the incense into the jar and label it accordingly.

Prosperity incense

Burn this incense whenever you are working prosperity magic.

What you need
A mortar and pestle, 3 tbsp dried mint, 5 dried bay leaves, 1 tsp dried basil, 3 drops patchouli oil, a clean jar, a label

What you do

- ✪ Put the mint, bay leaves, basil and patchouli oil in your mortar. Using the pestle and a deosil (clockwise) motion, grind the ingredients together, as you do so, imagining prosperity and abundance coming to you from all directions. Tell yourself all that you want is coming to you, and more. Keep your focus strong and clear.
- ✪ Once the incense is thoroughly mixed, transfer it to the jar and label it.

THE HEDGE WITCH'S KITCHEN

Pre-magic potion

When you work magic it is vital that you are in the right frame of mind. By taking a few moments for yourself and sipping the following potion, you can achieve the state of calm and collectedness that is essential for magic to take place.

What you need
Your favourite cup or mug, a camomile teabag (available from healthfood stores, herbalists and some supermarkets), 3 drops cherry plum Bach Flower Remedy, some sugar or honey

What you do
- ✪ Brew the camomile teabag in the cup, adding to it the cherry plum Bach Flower Remedy (to soothe and calm) and sugar or honey to taste.
- ✪ Sit in your kitchen and slowly sip the drink, thinking positively of the magic you are about to perform and focusing on your magical goal.
- ✪ When you have finished the potion, rinse out the mug and go about your chosen magical working.

Tasseomancy

Tasseomancy is the proper term for the art of tea-leaf-reading, which is a popular aspect of kitchen witching. In Victorian drawing rooms, tea-leaf-reading was almost a daily pastime. Although it is often ridiculed by modern society, tasseomancy is actually a form of scrying (or divination by seeing images in an object). But can a cup of tea really tell you your fortune?

While divination does have a role within the Craft, it is important to remember that to a large extent we shape our own future. Scrying in any form, including tea-leaf-reading, can give us an indication of where we are heading if we remain on the same life path and all factors remain unchanged. So if you don't like what you see in the leaves, or in any other form of divination, you might want to make some changes in your life! If tea-leaf-reading interests you, here's how to go about it ...

Reading the tea leaves

What you need
A dark tablecloth (a black velvet altar cloth is ideal, otherwise use a dark green or deep blue cloth), a teapot, some loose tea (not teabags), a trivet or table mat, a cup and saucer (make sure the cup has no pattern on the inside, as this could distract you when you are reading)

What you do
- ✪ Work out exactly what you want to know from the leaves.
- ✪ Set the scene by draping the cloth over your kitchen table. If you don't have a kitchen table, use a worktop.
- ✪ Brew up a pot of tea using the loose leaves. Stand the teapot on the trivet or table mat in the centre of the cloth. Allow the tea to steep for 10 to 15 minutes. While you are waiting, place the cup and saucer ready on the cloth.
- ✪ Pour the tea into the cup without using a tea strainer. Add a little milk if you really must – some witches believe that a divinatory tea should be drunk black – but do not add sugar, as this will affect the leaves and thus the reading.
- ✪ Sip your tea and ponder your question. Make sure you sip slowly and carefully so you don't choke on the tea leaves!
- ✪ When there is just a small amount of tea covering the leaves in the bottom of the cup, take the cup in your left hand and swirl it three times in a deosil (clockwise) direction, focusing hard on your chosen question. Now quickly tip the cup upside down onto the saucer and again turn it three times in a deosil direction.
- ✪ Pick up the cup and look at the patterns the leaves have made as they cling to the inside of the cup. Interpret the shapes using your own intuition or a good dictionary of dream symbols. The shapes closest to the cup handle are the influences of the near future, while those opposite the handle are symbolic of things that may occur at least six months to one year from the day of the reading. If you keep a Book of Shadows or herbal diary, make a note of your reading in it.

To invoke brownie blessings

The brownie is the elemental of the stove and the oven, and as a household spirit he can be called upon to guard and protect your sacred cauldron. Use this spell to invoke the elemental brownie of your kitchen, repeating it every full moon.

What you need
Your cauldron; a tray or plate; a saucer of milk, cream or honey; a sweet cake or biscuit, a picture or statue of a brownie (optional)

What you do

⭐ Stand at your cooker, with your – clean – cauldron on the hob. Hold your hands palms down over the cauldron and speak the following charm:

> *I call the brownie from below*
> *To guard this sacred cauldron.*
> *Protect this vessel from any foe*
> *And bless my sacred potions.*
> *So mote it be!*

⭐ Now place the tray or plate on the (unlit) hob next to the cauldron. Arrange on it the saucer of milk, cream or honey and the sweet cake or biscuit. This is your offering to your household brownie. Leave it in place for 24 hours for the elemental to take his psychic fill, then give the remains to the earth by placing them in the garden.

⭐ If you have a picture or a statue of a brownie, place it near your cooker.

Appliance magic

We rarely appreciate our modern appliances until something goes wrong with them! Then all of a sudden it becomes clear to us how easy they make our lives and how much we rely on them. By putting a little magic into our appliances, however, we can acknowledge the assistance they give us and the day-to-day convenience they provide.

To imbue smaller appliances, such a kettles and toasters, with magic, it is enough simply to hold them in your hands and say:

> *I dedicate this — (name appliance) as a magical tool.*
> *It is now a tool of the hedge witch.*
> *May it be powerful and reliable.*
> *So mote it be!*

You should repeat this ritual at least every three months, on the full moon.

For larger appliances, such as cookers, washing machines, dish washers, microwaves, fridge-freezers, vacuum cleaners and so on, you might like to perform the following ritual. Again, it should be repeated at least every three months, on the full moon.

THE HEDGE WITCH'S KITCHEN

To bless large appliances

What you need

A white candle, a stick of your favourite incense

What you do

⭐ Calm your mind and breathe deeply for a moment. Now light the candle and move it all around the exterior of your chosen appliance, saying as you do so:

> *I bless this — (name appliance) with the powers of fire.*
> *May it be a powerful, reliable and useful tool of this magical kitchen.*
> *So mote it be!*

⭐ Light the incense stick from the candle flame and move it all around the appliance (a technique known as smudging), saying as you do so:

> *I bless this — (name appliance) with the powers of smoke.*
> *May it be a powerful, reliable and useful tool of this magical kitchen.*
> *So mote it be!*

⭐ Work your way around the kitchen, blessing each appliance as you go. When you have finished, place the candle and incense on your kitchen altar to burn down.

Calling the pixies

Pixies are perfect elementals for the kitchen or dining room. They love joy and laughter and will bring these energies to your home. My own kitchen is filled with statues of cheeky pixies, and they bring a smile to the faces of all my visitors. These statues are widely available and very inexpensive, so you might like to begin a collection of your own. In my opinion, every kitchen should have at least one pixie statue!

Spell to call the pixies

If you're planning a dinner party or a gathering of some kind, perform this spell two hours before your guests are due to arrive and it should be a party to remember – for all the right reasons!

What you need
A pixie statue (optional)

What you do
- ✪ If you have a pixie statue, place it close by.
- ✪ As you light your kitchen altar candle, speak the following charm:

> *Pixies, I call you; hear this plea:*
> *Bring laughter and joy to my family and me.*
> *Pixies, I call you; gather here;*
> *Bring a swing to our party and fill us with cheer.*
> *Pixies, I call you; bring your love and your light;*
> *Empower this home with your magic so bright!*
> *So mote it be!*

Magical dining

There is much we can do to make an ordinary meal more magical. When you are chopping vegetables or making a sandwich, for example, use your pentagram chopping board. Focus your mind on the skills and power of the kitchen witch and fill the food with love, blessings and wishes for good health for your family.

Bless each dish you serve by drawing a pentagram in the air over it with a wooden spoon. Always remember to light your kitchen altar candle before you begin to work with food, and ask that the meal you prepare be good, tasty, wholesome and nutritious. Finally, set the table nicely and add a seasonal or magical touch, such as place mats decorated with leaf images, apple-style napkin rings, or candle-holders with a pentagram design. Just before you begin to eat, say a silent thank you to the Earth Goddess for providing such a bountiful feast for you and your loved ones to enjoy.

The dining room

If your house or flat has a separate dining room, there are ways in which you can enchant this space. If possible, have a round or oval dining table rather than a square or rectangular one. This will encourage a sense of equality among those gathered around it and will help to avoid confrontation at meal times. Place a figure of Demeter or a 'circle of friends' sculpture in the centre of the dining table.

Soft lighting and dark colours can greatly enhance a dining room, promoting an atmosphere of intimacy and sharing. Opt for earthy reds, deep pinks, shady violets and midnight blues. You can also bring in such magical themes as the fleur de lys or the five-pointed star. Choose accessories such as curtain poles, candlesticks and tableware carefully, making sure they tie in with your overall idea of what your magical home should look like and opting for those with the most magical designs. Like the kitchen, the dining room should reflect the turning wheel of the year, so bring in seasonal fruits, flowers and other decorations, and burn an appropriate oil.

Correspondences for the kitchen and dining room

Oils and incenses	Crystals	Angels	Elementals	Power animals
Spring	Clear quartz	Uriel	Salamander	Hen
Lilac	Snowy quartz		Sylph	Cow
Bluebell	Hematite		Brownie	Deer
Primrose	Aventurine		Pixie	Bee
Violet				Horse
Summer				
Sunflower				
Foxglove				
Rose				
Neroli				
Autumn				
Apple				
Pear				
Blackberry				
Oakmoss				
Winter				
Cinnamon				
Clove				
Ginger				
Pine				
Spice				

And So to Bed ...

Our bedrooms are much more than just places to sleep. It is here that we read, make love, dream, change our clothes and retreat into ourselves when things are going wrong in our lives.

Since earliest childhood, my bedroom has been my sanctuary, and although I've lived in many different homes, in all of them the bedroom has been the room that most reflected my personality. It was in the bedroom that I set up my first altar, performed my first spells and rituals, and wrote my first words for publication. It was in the bedroom that I lay sobbing and broken-hearted at the destruction of a relationship I had built my life around, and it is in my bedroom that I often reflect on the positive direction my life has taken since then. Many of you will have done similar things in your own bedroom.

In this chapter we are going to consider why this room is so central to our well-being and what we can do to fill it with magical, romantic, strengthening and nurturing vibrations. We will also be looking at how we can use the bedroom to increase the passion in our lives, and ways to overcome insomnia.

But first I want you to go up to your bedroom right now. Imagine that you are a stranger entering the room for the first time. What are your impressions? What thoughts immediately flit through your mind? Is the room beautiful and welcoming? Is it fresh and light? Does it speak to you of love, passion and romance? Is the atmosphere nurturing – do you feel safe here? Does the bed invite you to lie down, relax and dream? Take a good look around and make a note of any impressions you are not happy with. If you think the room looks cold and bare or is in need of redecorating, make a note of that. If it looks cluttered or is a dual purpose room (for example, your home office is in the corner or you live in a bedsit), you might want to jot down a few ideas for storage or for dividing the room up into different zones (perhaps using screens or bead curtains).

Once you have an honest view of your bedroom, compare it with the description you made of your ideal bedroom in your dream home book (see pages 28–30). How does your real room measure up to your ideal one? If there is a gap between the two, how can you bridge it? While this exercise may at first leave you a little disheartened, let me tell you that the first step to a great room is acknowledging the flaws (as well as the strengths) of what you already have. Remember that what you are seeking to re-create is the essence of your dream bedroom. With that in view, no matter how dismal your current circumstances may be, nothing is hopeless.

I know from experience that this is true – I went from having virtually nothing at the end of a relationship to sleeping in a beautiful four-poster bed in the heart of a fairytale boudoir. And all in less than two years. So, you see, it can be done, and you don't need a large fortune to do it either – just imagination, creativity, your time and a little magic!

The bed womb

Why is the bed such an important piece of furniture? Because it is our every-day womb. Only when we are tucked up in bed do we completely drop our guard, taking off the mask that we all wear in the outside world. When we are in bed asleep we are totally vulnerable, and yet it feels like the safest place there is. The mattress cushions our body, the pillows support our head and neck, the duvet or blankets fold around us, and we are embraced in womb-like warmth. Just as before birth we are nurtured and supported in the womb, so the bed nurtures us in our adult lives. It is where we rest after a long, hard day; where our skin is renewed and fed with nutrients; where our aching joints and tired muscles can finally relax; and where our bodies heal themselves as we peacefully sleep.

It is here, too, that we are shown the possibilities of our lives through the medium of dreams and that the fertility of the bed 'womb' invites us to make love. Is it any wonder that a small sigh of bliss often escapes us as we climb into bed or that we may have trouble getting up in the morning? Given the choice, I think most babies would stay in the womb if they could! And most of us have an overwhelming need to curl up in bed and let the world pass us by every now and then. Once you fully realise the significance of the bed, you will never look at bedtime in quite the same way again!

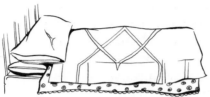

The enchanted boudoir

How you refer to your bedroom is of great magical importance, as words have power. You may call it your retreat, your sanctuary, your fairytale boudoir or your enchanted bower, but you must acknowledge the magical possibilities of the bedroom in some way in order to enchant this space. By changing how you refer to your bedroom you will change what you perceive it to be – and this in turn will help you to create the room of your dreams. This is true for any room in your house.

I used to call my spare room 'the junk room', as it was a storage space for unused furniture, Yuletide decorations and so on. Then I began to refer to it as 'my study', as this was what I wished it to become. Within a year the junk was cleared out and I had created a beautiful crimson study. So, you see, this simple technique really does work!

Choose your key words with care. They may relate to your dream home, in which case you might begin referring to your bedroom as 'the woodland grove', 'the country flower bower' or 'the sea siren's cove'. If you prefer, you can keep your key words private. They will function effectively as mental tags that you use to connect your room with your magic. If you are thinking of introducing a specific theme to your room – such as mermaids and sirens – you may find that people pick up on this without you having to say anything. On the other hand, you may find that declaring your intention for the room to family and friends will give you an added incentive to manifest it.

If you tell your family and close friends of your plans, they may help by looking out for perfect items for your theme or giving you extra-special birthday gifts. I told everyone of my intention to create a fairytale boudoir, and it was my mother who came across the four-poster bed and told me about it. This bed is now the main feature of my bedroom. You may even inspire those around you to create their own theme rooms – and so you will have helped, indirectly, to increase someone else's happiness.

When decorating your bedroom, choose soft colours but try to steer away from wishy-washy pastels. Go instead for a shade deeper to enhance the nurturing qualities of this room. Buy beautiful bed linen and matching or contrasting curtains, opting for luxurious fabrics such as velvet, silk, satin, chiffon and chenille to increase the soft womb-like feel of the bed. Add lots of boudoir cushions (these are the small rectangular ones), tasselled bolsters and throws in co-ordinating fabrics. Hang bead curtains and wind chimes in the windows to add the dimensions of light and sound. Wooden wind chines sound incredibly like cow bells, so if your dream home is the country cottage or the farmhouse, these are a must! If you want to live by the sea but your current home is firmly land locked, invest in a CD of ocean sounds and nod off to the gentle rhythm of the waves coming in to shore. Burn a sea mist oil or incense just before bed time and use sea shell necklaces as curtain tie-backs. Decorate in shades of blue, aqua and sea-green. You could invest in tables and cabinets fashioned to look like boats, lighthouses, sea-chests and mermaids – or build your own maritime furniture if you have the skills for it. Whatever your dream, make your bedroom – the place of dreams – reflect it.

Sleeping beauty

Choose your nightclothes with care. We all like to be comfortable, but nightwear should be sexy and glamorous too. Invest in slinky nightdresses of satin and lace, and short shifts in floral cotton. In winter, opt for satin pyjamas in jewel-like colours. If seduction is the name of the game, sheer black chiffon is generally a winner – put on a little natural make-up, soften the lights and spray on a beautiful, exotic perfume. Your man will soon rise to your bait!

Bedtime ritual

Creating a little ritual for yourself can go a long way towards getting a good night's sleep. Restful sleep is essential if we are to maintain our health and beauty and avoid the stress that is associated with sleep deprivation. By combining the following routine with the Candle Time one (see pages 75–6), you will be able to enjoy an evening of quiet relaxation and gentle activities designed to lull you into a state of peaceful slumber.

✪ The best way to begin your night-time routine is to take a long hot bath. The heated water will relax tired muscles, and stepping out of the bath will encourage the slight drop in body temperature that signals to your brain that it is time for sleep. Chapter 9 is full of ideas on how to make bathing more magical; choose some of these to incorporate into your nightly bedtime routine.

✪ Now that your pores have been opened by the heat of the bath, apply a lavender- or rose-scented body lotion to nourish your skin, and put a night cream on your face and neck to assist the skin's renewal process. Put on your glamorous Sleeping Beauty nightwear and prepare for bed.

✪ Prepare your boudoir by turning back the bed, lighting cosy lamps and scented candles, and spraying Slumber Spray (see page 102) around the room and on the bed linen. Play soothing music if you wish, or a CD of nature sounds. Choose a book or magazine and lay it ready on your bedside table.

✪ Finally, make up a slumber potion (see pages 102–3) and take it to bed with you (after checking the security of your home). Plump up the boudoir cushions and pillows, and sit in bed reading and relaxing until your potion is gone and your eyes begin to close. Sweet dreams!

To make slumber spray

Lavender is renowned for its ability to induce restful sleep. Spray this potion liberally onto bed linen while ironing, and spritz a little around your bedroom and on your duvet and pillow each night before retiring. This spray can also be used on your bedroom curtains. Open the window a little, allowing the night breeze to carry the fresh scent of lavender into your bedroom, inducing a night of peaceful sleep.

What you need
600 ml (1 pint) pure spring water (the bottled variety is fine), a saucepan, 10 drops lavender essential oil, 1 tbsp dried lavender, a clean spritzer bottle

What you do
- ✪ Pour the spring water into the saucepan. Add five drops of the lavender essential oil, together with the dried lavender heads. Simmer and stir for approximately 15 minutes.
- ✪ Allow the potion to cool and then add the remaining five drops of lavender essential oil. Transfer the potion, flower heads and all, into the spritzer bottle. Your Slumber Spray is now ready for use.

To make Milky Way slumber potion

What you need
A large mug (a latte mug is ideal), enough milk to fill the mug, a small saucepan or cauldron, 1 tsp golden honey, 2 drops rock rose Bach Flower Remedy, 2 drops gentian Bach Flower Remedy, some ground cinnamon

What you do
- ✪ Measure the milk into the mug and then transfer it to the saucepan or cauldron.
- ✪ Heat the milk gently, stirring in the honey once it has started to get warm.

- ⭐ Continue to heat the milk, stirring all the time, until it is just beginning to boil.
- ⭐ Pour the potion back into the latte mug. Add the rock rose and gentian Bach Flower Remedies, which have a soothing and relaxing effect. Sprinkle a little of ground cinnamon on top of the potion.
- ⭐ Take it to bed and enjoy!

To make luxury chocolate slumber potion

If, like me, you're a bit of a chocholic, you will love this slumber potion! Hot chocolate is a favourite bedtime drink. It contains an amino acid called tryptophan, which relaxes and induces sleep. This luxury chocolate potion is a truly decadent way to enter the Land of Nod!

What you need
A large mug of your favourite hot chocolate drink (the instant variety is fine), a saucepan or your cauldron, 3 squares of your favourite chocolate bar, 1 tbsp Tia Maria liqueur, 2 drops rock rose Bach Flower Remedy, 2 drops gentian Bach Flower Remedy

What you do
- ⭐ Prepare the hot chocolate as normal.
- ⭐ Transfer the hot chocolate to the saucepan or your cauldron and add the squares of chocolate. Heat very gently.
- ⭐ Once the chocolate squares have melted, add the Tia Maria, rock rose and gentian. Stir for another minute, then pour back into your mug.
- ⭐ Sip the potion in bed while relaxing with a good book.

Dream weaver

Most witches and magical practitioners keep a dream diary. This may be part of their personal diary, part of their Book of Shadows or a separate volume altogether. The reason for recording dreams is so that we can refer back to them. It then becomes easy to recognise when we have 'dreamed true' – which is an old country term for prophetic dreaming – and to link together the various signs and recurring symbols contained in our dreams in order to understand what they are trying to tell us. This latter practice is known as dream weaving.

We spend, on average, a third of our lives asleep, so it is essential to magical living that this time is recorded in some way, so that the messages of our night-time visions can be absorbed and acted upon. If dream weaving appeals to you, I suggest you buy a hard-bound notebook to use as your dream journal. You might also like to invest in a dictionary of dream symbols and interpretations – be aware, though, that you will often get a truer interpretation of your dreams by using your own intuition. For instance, the dream dictionary may tell you that your dream of a dog indicates a loyal friend; however, you are terrified of dogs, having been badly bitten as a child, and your intuition tells you to be on your guard as you may come under attack – or that it is time you faced your fears. In most cases, your first instinctive interpretation will be the correct one. So use a dictionary by all means, but remember that dream interpretations are not set in stone.

Keep your dream diary and a pen or pencil close by your bed. If you like, you can keep these items in a special box or bag. Quilted satin nightdress cases make pretty holders for dream weaving journals and are widely available from most department stores. Record your dreams each morning, making a note of the date, and keep a look out for any recurring dreams or symbols.

Before you use your dream diary, you should cleanse and bless it as a tool of your magic. If you are already keeping a dream diary and haven't already done this, don't worry; it's not too late to do it now. Try the following ritual.

To cleanse and bless a dream diary

This ritual uses a smudge stick, a traditional tool of psychic cleansing, generally made out of a bunch of dried sagebrush. Smudge sticks can be obtained from New Age stores.

What you need

A sagebrush smudge stick, your dream diary, your pentacle

What you do

- ✪ Light one end of the smudge stick so that it glows and smokes.
- ✪ Smoke your dream diary by passing the smudge stick all around it, as you do so, saying:

  I cleanse this book with the powers of Air, Earth and Fire.

- ✪ Lay the book on your pentacle. Hold your hands over it, palms down, and say:

  I empower this book as a magical tool and dedicate it to the realm of my dreams. May it be a true record of my dream time and a key to the mysteries I am endeavouring to learn. So mote it be!

- ✪ Leave the book on the pentacle for three days and three nights, after which is ready for use.

Moonbeams and dreams

The moon has a profound effect on our dreams, and also influences our sleeping patterns and the quality of our sleep. Most of us experience our most vivid dreams during the full moon. If you already make a practice of watching the cycle of the moon and recording your dreams, you may be aware that this is true for you. Try making a note of the moon phase in your dream diary and you will probably see a pattern emerging, with your most memorable, magical and occasionally disturbing dreams occurring at the time of the full moon.

This is especially the case if you sleep with the curtains open, allowing the moonbeams to spill across the room. Try it if you want to encourage strong dream visions. I have had two past-life dreams with the light of the full moon falling across my bed. Be aware, however, that not all of these nocturnal journeys are pleasant.

You can encourage prophetic dreams by placing your bed with the head in the west, the direction of psychic abilities, dreams, magic, intuition and increased awareness. Sleeping with your head in the west opens the gates to the psychic realms. Your subconscious mind will soak up what it finds there, and this new-found knowledge will often manifest itself in your dreams.

We are more susceptible to bad dreams, nightmares and the night terrors during the time of the waning moon. Hanging a magical charm such as a dream-catcher or a small round mirror above the head of the bed can help to ease the unpleasantness of such dreams and may even keep them away altogether. However, if there is a specific message for you within a certain nightmare, you will keep experiencing it until you finally get the point! Your dream diary will help you to see such messages more quickly, thus saving you from nights of unnecessarily disturbed sleep.

Another way to protect yourself during sleep is to place a traditional witch's besom, or broomstick, beneath the bed. The bristles should point towards the bedhead. This is an ancient protection rite of the wise woman, and may stem from the Burning Times (the persecution of witches in the 16th and 17th centuries), when to be found in possession of a broom meant almost certain death – even though every household had one! Sprinkling a small amount of sea-salt around the bed is also said to protect you during sleep and will ward off all negativity – including bad dreams. My favourite protection charm, however, is a talisman featuring a witch and the moon. These are available from New Age stores and should be hung above the bed to watch over you as you sleep. An angel charm will also do the trick, and may be more acceptable if you live with non-witchy folk!

AND SO TO BED ...

Making a dream pillow

Lavender-filled dream pillows can be bought from many garden centres, gift shops and department stores, but they are easy to make. This pillow will induce restful sleep and psychic dreams.

What you need

A piece of pretty fabric large enough to make a small pillow (many fabrics are suitable, but felt and velvet are both easy to sew and pleasant to lie on); equal parts of dried lavender, dried camomile and dried mugwort in a sufficient quantity to stuff your pillow; lace and ribbons for trimming

What you do

- ✪ Sew the fabric into a basic pillow shape, leaving one end open for stuffing.
- ✪ Stuff your pillow with the lavender (for sleep), camomile (for relaxation) and mugwort (for psychic dreams).
- ✪ Sew up the remaining side of the pillow, and trim the pillow with the lace and ribbons.
- ✪ Place the magical pillow on your bed, on top of your ordinary pillow, and look forward to meaningful dreams.

Wish upon a star

The practice of wishing upon a star will probably be familiar to you from childhood, but no chapter on bedroom magic would be complete without it. I have been wishing upon stars since I was a small girl, and I am thankful that I have never grown out of this night-time ritual. I often wish upon the constellation of Orion, as I see Orion as the Knight of Night and a granter of my deepest wishes. (For a love spell based on Orion, see Prince of Stars on page 110.) You can wish on any constellation you feel an affinity with, or you can use the traditional technique of wishing on the first star you see each night. If you choose the latter, recite the following popular rhyme as you focus on the star and then make your wish:

Star light, star bright,
First star I see tonight,
I wish I may, I wish I might
Have the wish I make this night.

I have a star-fairy music box that plays 'When You Wish Upon a Star'. I like to set it playing as I make my wish, thus empowering the magic with music. Many children's jewellery boxes play this tune, so it's quite easy to get hold of one if you like the idea of spelling to music. Remember to make your wish from the heart and keep it to yourself. Share your wish with the stars and wait for it to come true!

Love and romance

The bedroom is the centre-stage for our passionate encounters. Even if you're single, you may find that your thoughts turn to an unknown love as you lie awake at night.

Magical bedrooms should reflect this important aspect of life, whether you are madly in love, happy to remain single for the time being, or involved in a relationship that is less than you would wish for. If you are married or in a relationship, your bedroom can be used as a magical tool to help keep the passion and romance flowing. In this section of the book, we will be looking at a variety of ideas for gaining the most from this intimate aspect of the bedroom.

The love altar

Every bedroom should have some form of love altar. This can be as elaborate or as discreet as you like, as long as it acknowledges in some way the vibrations that bedrooms inevitably generate. In setting up an altar that is specifically dedicated to love, you are inviting more love into your life. If you are single, this may lead to a new love walking into your life or the return of an old flame. Or it may set off a new spark in an established relationship.

Even if you are heart-broken following a romantic disappointment and feel that it's safer to be alone, it is important not to cut yourself off completely from this aspect of life. Although you will need time to heal, you might like to look back at your early romantic ideals and build an altar around them. If you like, you can keep the altar strictly within the realm of the arts, using pictures of knights in armour, for example, or a copy of *Romeo and Juliet* with a red candle beside it. In this way you are acknowledging that love is still out there, that it is still a possibility and that there is a place in your life for love when the time is right for you to try again with someone new.

Whatever your current circumstances and romantic goals for the future, the basics of a love altar are the same. Choose a sturdy surface – a small table or window sill are both ideal – and arrange upon it red and pink candles in suitable holders, and tea-lights in holders fashioned to look like (or decorated with) hearts. Add an oil-burner – perhaps one with a cherub design – and burn oils associated with love and passion, such as ylang ylang and rose. Red roses and scattered rose petals are symbolic of true love; oyster shells symbolise passion and lust; and ivy stands for fidelity. Any of these could be included on your love altar.

Add figures of loving couples, especially if you're single and looking for a new love. If you're married or in a committed relationship, place a photograph of the two of you in the centre of the altar. If you are currently getting over a break-up, are feeling the pangs of unrequited love (which can be just as painful) or are suffering some other kind of romantic disappointment, add symbols of healing to your love altar, such as a figure of the healing goddess Kuan Yin, a dolphin or a blue floating candle in a bowl of water. In magic both the element of water and the colour blue are associated with strong powers of healing.

If you are trying to start a family, add symbols of fertility to your bedroom altar – a bowl of seeds, acorns, pine cones, a figure or picture of a rabbit, or even a statue of a magical moon hare (available from some Wiccan shops and websites).

Make your love altar reflect who you are, your current circumstances and your dreams for the future. Spend a few moments here every day. Light the candles, burn oils or incense and reflect on where your love life is going, expressing what it is that you actually want. Too often we leave love to chance and then wonder why it all goes wrong! Sometimes fate needs a helping hand, so don't be afraid to pursue your destiny. Take control of your love life and direct it towards your future happiness. The energies you create with this love altar will magically enchant your bedroom, and you should notice a significant improvement in your relationships in due course.

Prince of Stars love spell

This spell is designed to bring a new love into your life (or bring back an old flame). It uses the night sky as a focus, so you will need to work it outside or at a window from which you can see the constellation of Orion, the prince among the stars! Repeat the spell nightly until your true love comes into your life.

What to do

⚝ Focus on Orion and think of your ideal love or old flame. Breathe deeply and then chant the following charm three times:

> *Knight of Night, Prince of Stars,*
> *May true love soon be ours.*
> *Knight of Night, of stars that shine,*
> *May true love soon be mine.*
> *Orion, in the stars you glow,*
> *Stirring thoughts of a love I used/I've yet to know.*
> *Be he near or be he far,*
> *Let him come now and find his Little Star!*

Romance of roses spray

This spray will induce a night of love and romance. Spritz it liberally on the bed linen and all around the bedroom.

What you need
600 ml (1 pint) pure spring water (the bottled variety is fine), your cauldron, 5 tbsp rose water, 5 drops rosewood essential oil, 4 drops ylang ylang essential oil, a few dried rose petals (pink or red), a wooden spoon, a spritzer bottle, a label

What you do
✪ Pour the pure spring water into your cauldron. Add the rose water, three drops of the rosewood essential oil, two drops of the ylang ylang essential oil and the rose petals. Stir deosil (clockwise) and simmer for 10–15 minutes.

✪ Allow to cool, then add the remaining two drops of rosewood oil and two drops of ylang ylang oil.

✪ Transfer to a spritzer bottle, label and use as desired.

You sexy witch!

To spice up a flagging love life why not turn your bedroom into a sexy witch's boudoir and playroom?

Bring in lots of deep reds in the form of flowers, cushions, throws and so on – or decorate the room in shades of warm, earthy red. Have your Wiccan altar on full display in the bedroom. There's something about witchcraft that even the most sceptical of men are intrigued by – and tradition states that once a man has kissed or made love to a witch, he will never forget her and never get over her ... so do treat the boys nicely, won't you girls?

If a four-poster bed is out of the question, then invest in a bed canopy. These are quite inexpensive and come in various jewel-like colours and pastel shades. By the bed, place a bottle of wine or champagne, two glasses and a bowl of fruit or goodies. Lots of mirrors will reflect candlelight, enhancing the seduction theme you're going for. Be careful not to overdo it, though, as that could scare him off! Think subtle seduction and enchantment!

At the bottom of the bed you could place a 'toy box' – a locked trunk filled with love potions, massage oils and perhaps one or two, er ... unmentionable items. I'll leave that bit to your imagination! Add a small shelf or bookcase filled with volumes on love spells, love potions and massage techniques, as well as erotic fiction and sex manuals. Include a pretty bag or box filled with condoms so you're always prepared (and protected), even if he isn't! Hey presto, you're one super, sexy witch! Enjoy, enchant and be safe.

Correspondences for the bedroom

Oils and incenses	Crystals	Angels	Elementals	Power animals
Rose	Amethyst	Michael	Undine	Owl
Jasmine	Rose quartz	Uriel		Bat
Ylang ylang	Moonstone	Raphael		Cat
Patchouli	Sodalite	Gabriel		Winged horse
Strawberry				Snake
Frankincense				
Lavender				

Magical Bathing

As the bathroom is usually the smallest room of the house, it is often difficult to use it to its full potential, with the result that it becomes a neglected space. While it can be hard to see the magic of the wash basin and the toilet, in the witch's house the bathroom is full of enchantment! Here banishing spells are written on tissues and flushed down the loo, healing potions are added to the bath water, and hair rinses are applied over the wash basin.

As the prime element of the bathroom is, obviously, Water, it is often decorated in shades of blue, aquamarine and sea-green, while an ocean theme of sea shells and starfish is sometimes brought in too. In choosing this kind of decor, people are unconsciously tapping into the magic of this room. On some level they are aware of the element and elementals of Water. I wonder how many of you reading this have some form of ocean theme in your bathroom. Dolphins, whales, fish, sea shells, mermaids, starfish, seahorses and so on regularly find their way into people's homes and take up residence in the bathroom.

Many modern design books will tell you that this look is outdated and lacks imagination, but design, like fashion, is based on fads. Magic, on the other hand, is based on the tangible energies of the natural world around us and its elemental powers. In the magical home, therefore, a bathroom with a sea theme is perfect for enhancing the magic that will take place there. It will also help to enhance the magic of the room on a daily basis.

If the sea isn't really your thing, look to other bodies of water for inspiration. Consider introducing a river theme, for example, in which the energies are softer and gentler than those of the ocean. You could decorate in shades of green and have a green voile blind or bead curtain at the window, filtering the light into the room and giving it a riverside hue. Hang pictures of river scenes, kingfishers and so on, and place a vase of bulrushes by the bath. Dragonfly wind chimes, a swan-shaped soap-dish and scented candles fragranced with riverside plants or wild flowers would all help to complete the effect.

If a river theme doesn't appeal either, how about taking your inspiration from the Scottish lochs and glens and using shades of green, granite and slate-grey, with a touch of heather-pink? Or think of an Arctic fjord or Icelandic lagoon, picking pale blues, whites and silvers for your decor. Flick through some holiday brochures for ideas and use your imagination. Remember that just because something hasn't been done before in any of your friends' houses, that doesn't mean it's not a good idea. Be the first and start a trend!

Once you have your basic decoration and colour palette completed, you will need to think about storage. Bathrooms have a bad habit of attracting clutter, with cosmetics, medicines and toiletries spilling out of cabinets and over surfaces. First of all, throw out anything that's past its use-by date. Sort everything else into wicker baskets or your chosen form of storage. Stow away anything that you don't use on a daily basis. Now place a pretty oil-burner or censer in a corner and arrange lots of candles in holders that match your theme and decor. You are now ready to make magic!

Moon bathing

One of the most magical ways to enhance your bath is to bathe by moonlight – particularly the light of the full moon.

What you need
A white or silver candle and a suitable holder, your cauldron, 3 drops lily of the valley essential oil

What you do
- ⭐ Switch all the lights off and, if you can, allow the moonbeams to spill into the bathroom. Light the white or silver candle.
- ⭐ Run your bath as usual, but do not add bath salts or foams.
- ⭐ Once your bath is full, dip in your cauldron and take some of your bath water out into the light of the moon. Stand your cauldron so that the full moon is reflected in the surface of the water and say:

> *As the moon is bright for all to see,*
> *I take its beauty into me.*

- ⭐ Carry the cauldron back into the bathroom and pour the moon-charged water back into the bath. Add the lily of the valley essential oil and enjoy your bath.

Moontime

'Moontime' is the term witches use to refer to their menstrual period. We see this as a most magical time, and while we may experience cramps and discomforts like everyone else, we try to accept these as part of the magic of our cycle. Our periods connect us to the moon itself, to the earth and to the greater story of life. Down the centuries, however, women in our culture have been taught that periods are a curse, and even that they are dirty. This, of course, is simply not true. Periods are the essence of life-giving creation, and that in itself is pure magic.

Most women feel a little out of sorts during their period, and may need some extra TLC from others and a large measure of self-love.

However, many women also admit to feeling at their sexiest during moontime. This can lead to incredible frustration, as we are encouraged to believe that we should not engage in sex at this time. However, there is no biological reason why this should be so.

During our moontime we may feel the need to withdraw from people and retreat into ourselves for a few days. This need for quietness and alone time is completely natural; in some tribal societies in the past, a special women's tent or lodge was erected for this very purpose. Modern Western women, however, are expected to carry on as normal, working a full-time job, looking after children and taking care of the household chores. This pressure can add to the stresses of this time of the month. While advertisements for sanitary products insist on telling us that our periods need not interfere with our daily lives, witches know that our periods are *supposed* to interfere with our daily lives. It is modern patriarchal society that denies us this right.

As the bathroom is often the most private place in a family household, take some time to yourself and enjoy a moontime retreat there, using some of the suggestions on the following pages.

Moontime bathing

Geranium and raspberry – which feature in this ritual – have long been used by wise women to ease the symptoms of PMT and painful periods respectively. Drinking raspberry tea during the three days leading up to and throughout your moontime will help to reduce menstrual cramps and reduce excessive bleeding. (If you have sensitive skin, make sure that geranium oil will not irritate it before you add this oil to your bath.)

What you need
10 drops geranium essential oil, a raspberry teabag (available from healthfood stores and most supermarkets), sugar or honey to sweeten your tea

What you do
✪ Run your bath as usual and add the geranium essential oil.
✪ Use the raspberry teabag and sugar or honey to brew yourself a cup of tea.
✪ Take this tea to the bathroom with you and sip it as you enjoy a long relaxing bath. Allow the healing water to ease your cramps and pains, and try to accept the sacredness of your moontime.

Moontime massage oil

Try using this oil to massage your stomach and lower back during your moontime, perhaps after Moontime Bathing above. It will help to relieve cramps. (If you have sensitive skin, make sure that geranium oil will not irritate it before you use this oil.)

What you need
1 tsp sweet almond oil, 3 drops geranium massage oil

What you do
✪ Pour the sweet almond oil into your hand and add the geranium essential oil. Use it to massage your stomach and lower back in a deosil (clockwise) direction on a daily basis.

Magical baths

Having a bath can be a ritual in its own right. Try the following suggestions to introduce a little magic into your bath-time routine.

Skin-care bath

The milk in this potion will soften the bath water and leave your skin feeling smooth and silky, while scenting it with the warm fragrance of vanilla.

What you need
2 tbsp dried milk, 5 drops vanilla essential oil

What you do

✪ When you have run your bath, sprinkle the dried milk into it. Mix the water well – it will go a lovely milky white colour. Add the vanilla essential oil.

✪ If you have long hair, tie it up, then bathe as usual.

Prosperity bath

This ritual should be carried out on the night of the new moon.

What you need
A mint tea bag, a handful of sea-salt, 3 silver coins, a green candle

What you do

✪ Hang the mint teabag over the hot tap so that the water flows over it as you run your bath, releasing the potency of the herb. Add the sea-salt and silver coins to the bath water.

✪ Light the candle and place it at the end of the bath, where you can focus on it.

✪ Now relax in the magical bath water and fix your gaze on the candle, strongly visualising the prosperity and abundance you wish to enjoy.

✪ When your focus is strong, begin to chant a prosperity chant. You can either write one of your own or use the following:

> *All I want is coming to me;*
> *I welcome the gift of prosperity.*

✪ Wash your face, body and hair with the magical bath water, literally washing the power of prosperity over yourself.

✪ When you have finished bathing, fish out the three coins and keep them safely – do not spend them. Pull out the plug to release your magic into the universe. Keep the candle with you and allow it to burn down naturally. If you have to interrupt your work, make sure you blow out the candle and light it again as soon as you can to complete the spell.

Healing bath

This bath is great if you're feeling a little off colour, and it will also help you to de-stress after a hard day.

What you need
Some candles and suitable holders, your favourite incense, 3 tbsp lavender water, 10 drops lavender essential oil

What you do
✪ Create a relaxing mood by lighting the candles and dotting them around the bathroom. Light the incense and then run a hot bath.

✪ Add the lavender water and lavender essential oil.

✪ Lie back in the water and allow the healing scent of lavender to wash over you and relax you completely.

Cosmetics

Cosmetics have been part of our lives since ancient times. They were in fact first used for magical purposes rather than to enhance the appearance, as is generally the case today. Most people are aware of the Ancient Egyptians' passion for eye make-up, but did you know that this was intended to ward off the evil eye? Green and blue eye shadows were applied as a personal protection device, and also to prevent blindness, while lip colour was used to prevent the soul escaping through the mouth and to guard against food poisoning.

We can use make-up in a similar way by applying it with a magical intent. You might, for example, use a little glitter or body shimmer to make you shine at a party in the metaphorical sense, or you might apply your mascara with the intent of catching someone's eye. Alternatively, try empowering a lipstick or lip balm using one of the following spells.

Lip balm enchantment for public speaking

If you are giving a speech, or even if you just need to have a chat with your boss or face some kind of confrontation, try this spell.

What you need
A new lip balm

What you do

- Take the lip balm to a quiet place and hold it in your hands. Visualise the lip balm absorbing a magical white light.
- Now see yourself saying all that you need to say, politely, clearly and with strength. Know that your words will flow easily and that you will be able to keep any nerves under control. See yourself speaking in a low, steady rhythm, without tripping over your words.
- When you have finished empowering the lip balm in this way, apply some and practise your speech.
- Just prior to your speaking engagement, reapply the lip balm at least three times. All will go well.

Red lipstick enchantment for kissable lips

Red is the colour of love and passion, and as it comes in many different shades, there will be a lipstick out there that suits you perfectly.

What you need
A new lipstick

What you do
- ✪ Hold the lipstick in your hands. Visualise your lips acting as magnets. See yourself kissing your chosen partner and know that your lips are irresistible.
- ✪ When you have completed the visualisation, carefully apply the lipstick and wait for its magic to work.

Rose rinse of attraction

This hair rinse is one of my favourite beauty spells. I've been using it for years. It's a great way to get yourself noticed as you're out and about – men will feel the compelling need to comment on the fragrance of your hair!

What you need
A bottle of rosewater, a washing-up bowl, a jug

What you do
- ✪ Wash your hair. Pour the water for the final rinse into the washing-up bowl and add two capfuls of rosewater.
- ✪ Using the jug, rinse your hair, repeatedly pouring the scented water over it until it is lightly fragranced. Allow your hair to dry naturally.
- ✪ Each morning, pour a little rose water into the palm of your hand, rub your hands together and then run them through the entire length of your hair to renew the rose fragrance.

Siren song to attract a lover

This is an adaptation of a spell that first appeared in my book *Magical Beasts*.

What you need
An image or statue of a mermaid or siren (optional)

What you do
- Take the mermaid or siren representation to the bathroom – or simply visualise a mermaid or siren. Run yourself a bath.
- As you lie in the bath, focus on your mermaid or siren and say:

> *Beautiful siren, enchantress and seductress, I ask that you bestow your gifts upon me that I may attract love and passion into my life. Be with me and assist me in my magical working.*

- Now focus on your chosen love – this may be your current partner or it may be your ideal lover. Feel the mermaid or siren's energies around you and imagine that you are absorbing them into yourself. You are becoming a siren.
- When you feel ready, chant the following siren song three times, maintaining a clear visualisation of your love as you do so:

> *Come to me; I summon thee;*
> *Hear now my siren song.*
> *Come to me; I summon thee,*
> *For I have loved thee long.*
> *Swim with me; spin with me;*
> *Live with me and be my love.*
> *Play with me; lie with me;*
> *I'll take you to the stars above.*
> *Dance with me; entranced you'll be;*
> *I cast my witch's web out wide.*
> *Think of me; dream of me;*
> *From my charms you cannot hide.*

Look for me; feel for me;
The magic of my spell unfurls.
Teach me and reach out for me;
My love for you will rock your world.
Let me lead you by the hand
To my secret place.
Your will succumbs to my demand,
Crossing time and space.
See my lips, my swaying hips;
Your gaze is locked with mine.
Feel my power; 'tis the hour;
Come now – you are mine!

Correspondences for the Bathroom

Oils and incenses	Crystals	Angels	Elementals	Power animals
Sea mist	Sodalite	Raphael	Undine	Dolphin
Ocean breeze	Blue lace agate	Gabriel		Whale
Rose	Moonstone			Seahorse
Lavender	Amber			All aquatic animals
Citrine	Amethyst			

A Study of Magic

In the past, the study, or library, was a masculine domain. It was to this room that the gentlemen would retire after dinner to smoke pipes, drink brandy, discuss politics and business, and contemplate life. The ladies, of course, would gather in the drawing room to discuss needlepoint and philanthropy! Such was the role of the study in the past. In modern times, however, this room is enjoying a revival, and along with it a new character. With more and more people opting to work from home, a study is once again becoming essential, and even the smallest spaces are being converted into home offices.

But even if you don't work from home, there are many reasons to create a study. First of all, a study provides a quiet area for thinking, reading or just escaping from the distraction of the TV, stereo and telephone. If you have children, providing a small retreat for them to sit quietly doing homework and school projects may help them to concentrate. Having the PC in a communal study rather than in the privacy of a child's bedroom will also enable you to keep an eye on them when they use the Internet, which is full of hidden dangers that children are often unaware of. A small study also provides a space for filing household accounts neatly in a desk drawer, filing cabinet or set of pigeon holes, making it easy to see which bills and so on need your immediate attention.

Since I am a bookworm, the idea of a study has always appealed to me. A room totally dedicated to books, knowledge, learning, writing and reading is my idea of heaven. It is something that I have longed for since childhood and has been a longstanding feature of my dream home. But I have only recently had the time to create a study within my current home. As this is my fifth book, I decided it was time to take my writing more seriously and dedicate a space to my work, so I set about turning the spare room into a cosy little study. I spent a week up to my elbows in deep-red paint, curtain poles, voile blinds and bookcases that came with the inscription every single girl dreads: 'Requires home assembly'!

But the end result was totally worth the effort. Now all my books are in one room, arranged by category in mahogany bookcases. My word processor stands ready on a small desk, and a beautiful Chippendale escritoire stands before the window. This study completely fulfils my requirements as a writer. Everything I need is within easy reach. It is a quiet room at the back of the house overlooking the garden, so there are no distractions. As there are no clocks, telephones or TVs, it is a space out of time, allowing me to drift wherever my writing takes me.

You may or may not have an available room to turn into a study, but perhaps you can dedicate part of another room to this purpose, possibly partitioning it off with curtains, screens or free-standing bookcases. Remember, the important thing is not how much space you have but how you use it to capture the essence of your dream study.

The essence of your dream study may be completely different from mine. Think about what your needs are and what you plan to do in this room, and that will help you to create the vision. If you are a bookworm, you will need plenty of bookcases, or at least a set of sturdy shelves. If you have children, a table that can seat several people may be more practical than a desk, as your kids can then work together or invite friends round to study with them. If you work from home, you will probably want to set up your PC in the study, and if you're going to spend a lot of time in your study – as most home-workers do – you will want to install a coffee-maker or a kettle! A desk chair that supports your back and is adjustable in height is also a must.

If you plan to keep important documents, emergency household cash, bills and so on in the study, you will need to think about security. A cupboard or drawer that locks will serve for most homes – but don't make the mistake that many people do and leave the key in the lock! If you plan to run a home-based business and will have lots of cash and valuables on the premises, you should invest in some sort of safe.

When decorating your study, try to pick deep, warm colours. My own study is a deep berry-red, which has a very earthy tone. You might prefer aubergine, midnight blue, cinnamon or forest green. Then again, you may opt for a more modern look, choosing chrome and glass furniture and painting the walls silver or pewter-grey. Go for whatever appeals to you.

You may choose to create a study entirely for magical purposes. In this case you could take inspiration from the alchemists of old, who lined their studies with ancient magical tomes, spell books, almanacs, astrological charts and maps of the heavens. Choose a magical deep-purple colour scheme, dark wood furniture that is intricately carved and rich purple velvets. Place your Book of Shadows on an ornate bookstand or music stand, and add a telescope for gazing at the night sky, a microscope for studying the intricacies of the natural world and a large crystal ball or dark scrying mirror. Figures of gargoyles and dragons, rich tapestries and fake wood panelling will all help to bring an air of the alchemist's magic to your home study. Use your imagination and get creative. There are no limits to what you can do and the look you can achieve. Just be brave, throw out that magnolia emulsion and go for it!

Owl wisdom

Every study should have an owl. As creatures of knowledge and wisdom, owls are the perfect familiar for this room. They can be represented in pictures, statues, wood carvings and so on.

What you need
A small figure of an owl (chose him with care, making sure that you can see the wisdom of the species within the figure); pens, pencils or a packet of paper clips

What you do
- Take your owl figure to your desk and place him in the centre. Now create a magic circle around him, using the pens, pencils or a string of the paper clips.
- Once the circle is complete and the owl within, hold your hand over the him, palms down, and repeat the following charm three times:

Owl of wisdom,
Great thoughts you sow;
Help my mind to grow.
Owl of wisdom,
Bird of night,
Let my thoughts take flight.
Owl of wisdom,
Let me find
Clarity in my mind.
Owl of wisdom,
Let me see
The wisdom within me.

★ Take down the circle and find a home for the owl on your desk. He will keep your thoughts flowing and your mind clear.

Getting organised

One of the keys to organisation is storage. Having a place for everything and keeping everything in its place will in turn make you feel more in control of your life. Lack of good organisation can be the cause of an unpaid bill or your child not being able to go on a school trip because you lost the consent form you were supposed to sign!

If you want to get more organised, start by having a really good clear-out. Invest in some attractive storage boxes, sticky labels and a desk-top paper shredder. Shred everything that is out of date or of no further use to you – junk mail should always be shredded immediately! File away bank statements, paid bills and so on. Put important documents such as birth certificates, passports, mortgage papers, and car and house insurance policies into a separate storage box. Label all the boxes as you fill them, and put them safely on a shelf or in a cupboard. Even your wardrobe will do if you have no other space – just make sure you know where to find them!

Finally, if your desk has pigeon holes, use them to file unpaid bills, essential addresses, letters from school and so on. If there are no pigeon holes, buy a desk-top organiser from a stationer's and use this instead.

When you can actually see how many bills are in the 'unpaid' compartment, you may find you are induced to pay them more promptly!

Keeping household accounts

I know it may seem like an old-fashioned idea, but keeping a household accounts book can really help you to organise your finances. While most of us have an idea of what our household bills come to each month, and we can generally say how much we need to earn as a basic survival budget, few of us are aware of how much we spend on extras – the odd treat now and then, things for the kids, take-aways and so on. In fact, these all add up to a lot more than we like to think.

If you begin to write down everything you spend, you will soon build up an accurate picture of where your money is going – and there may be one or two nasty surprises! You may discover, for instance, that you spend a small fortune on cappuccinos or that your love of designer perfumes is costing you a king's ransom!

Start today. Get an A4 notebook and divide it into columns. You will need a column for each type of expenditure you have – for example, groceries, clothes, sweets and chocolate, and so on – as well as a column for making a more detailed note of what the expenditure was. Write down everything you spend in the relevant column. At the end of the week, add up each column. At the end of the month, add them up again. This will show you exactly what you do with your money – and maybe how and where it could be better spent.

You will find that your accounts book comes in useful if you need to save for something special or make cut-backs due to financial problems. Doing your accounts may not be the most exciting way to spend an evening, but it will put you more in control of your expenditure and help you to steer your finances in the right direction.

Gargoyle guardian

Many of us keep a small sum of cash handy in the home in case of emergencies, and this is a good idea, providing it is kept securely in a cash box and you're the only person who knows about it. If you have cash – or credit cards and the like – locked away at home, it is a good idea to invoke a guardian to protect the cash box where you keep it.

What you need
A small figure of a gargoyle, a piece of black cloth large enough to wrap around the cash box, a little sea-salt

What you do
⭐ Take all the above items to your household altar. Lay the black cloth out and place the cash box in the centre. Sprinkle it with a little sea-salt, as you do so, saying:

Protected be!

⭐ Place the gargoyle on top of the cash box and say:

Magical gargoyle, guard and protect all I place within this box. So mote it be!

⭐ Wrap the black cloth around both the gargoyle and cash box, tying them up in a bundle and placing them somewhere safe. The spell is complete.

Avoiding debt

With credit being so readily available, it's not surprising that many people are suffering the stress of debt. It has been speculated that almost everyone in the UK has some kind of debt, be it a mortgage, a credit card bill, a loan for a car, or goods bought from a catalogue on credit. But we all have to pay back what we owe at some stage in life. It's all well and good if the 'buy now, pay later' scenario catches up with you when your life is running smoothly and you have a good job, but how do you cope in times of hardship? How do you avoid borrowing more to pay what you already owe, and how do you keep your home safe from the creditors?

Well, the first thing to remember is that you are not alone. People up and down the country are in exactly the same situation, so don't panic! Keep a cool head and know that most companies who offer credit are aware of the problems that can arise with repayments and are willing to accept reduced amounts until you get back on your feet financially. A quick phone call is usually all it takes, so be brave and ring all your creditors. Explain the situation to them and see if you can come to a new arrangement.

That done, turn your attention to a little magical protection ...

Spell to avoid debt

What you need
A small box, a length of black ribbon, an obsidian crystal, some black pepper, a slip of paper and a pen, a small plastic tub

What you do

⭐ Take the box, the ribbon, the crystal and the black pepper to your desk or the place where you keep your bills. Bundle all your debt papers together and tie them with the black ribbon, as you do so saying:

I banish these debts from my life.

⭐ Put the papers in the box, together with the obsidian crystal, which will absorb the negativity attached to the debt. Scatter a little black pepper over the top. This will help to banish these particular bills. Close the box and put it in a dark place.

⭐ Write down the total amount that you owe on the slip of paper and put this in the plastic tub. Fill the tub with water, put on the lid and place it in the freezer – this will magically freeze your debt and will prevent it getting any bigger. However, you must back this up by cutting up credit cards, throwing away catalogues and so on.

⭐ Scatter a little black pepper around the perimeter of your home to banish debt from your property. Continue to make the new payments you've arranged to clear your debts.

Creativity in the study

As well as the centre of household finances, the study is usually a place for creativity. It may be where your children work on school projects and essays, or where you or your partner work or write journals, letters, reports and so on. Perhaps you are working on your own book right now, or have plans to begin a novel or a screenplay. If you are an artist, perhaps your study is also your studio.

Whatever your creative ambitions, you can enchant your study to assist the creative process and magnetise success. The spells in this section are not just for serious writers; they can be used by anyone, regardless of their individual ambitions. If you are a would-be poet or a student working on a thesis, calling your muse can help your work to flow freely. If you need to revise for an exam, get your homework done or draw up a new domestic budget, a spell for concentration will be of assistance.

Whatever your creative goal, setting the scene and preparing thoroughly are essential. A familiar routine for starting work will signal to your brain that it's time to let the creative juices flow. Most writers have little rituals they perform and objects they like to have around them as they work. While some people prefer to work directly onto the computer, others – myself included – find that the keyboard creates a block. I write all my books and articles in the old-fashioned way, using pen and paper, and then transfer them onto disk once the creative process is over. J.K. Rowling, author of the Harry Potter series, writes this way too – an indication that doing things in the traditional way is certainly no block to success!

It's a good idea to collect everything you need before you begin to work, so reference books, study guides, paints, calculators and so on should all be close to hand. However, they should not be allowed to clutter your work space. A bookstand is useful if you are a writer or a student. If you plan to be at your desk for a while, make sure you have a good supply of tea, coffee or mineral water. Tell people you don't wish to be disturbed, and start work.

To bring a little magic to your work, light a candle and place it on your desk (being careful to keep it out of the way of papers and other flammable objects). Burn an uplifting oil such as grapefruit or lemon balm. Have one or two nic-nacs close by to inspire you and remind you of your ultimate goal. On my desk, for instance, I have a bronze lamp in the form of a faerie, whose wings are made of tiffany glass. She reminds me of the magical powers of earth and the elemental powers about which I write. I also have an incense-holder fashioned as a sorceress, a picture of the goddess Epona, a faerie oil-burner and a frosted-glass tea-light holder in the shape of a fairytale castle. This last was a gift from my mother. I light it whenever I am writing, because it inspires me to keep going and connects me with the ultimate goal of my dream house. All the items on my desk remind me of magic and witchcraft and so link that realm of enchantment with my work as a writer. See if you can find a few things to place around you as you work. If you think carefully, you may notice that you already have one or two treasures that could be placed on your desk to inspire as you strive to achieve your creative ambitions.

Once you've set the scene and collected all you need, use any of the following spells to magically enchant your creativity.

Spell to call your muse

We all have a muse. For this spell you will need to find a picture or statue that represents yours. The identity of your muse is a very personal thing, and there are no right and wrong images. A muse doesn't have to be an ethereal or fairy-like being, although she can be. If you are working on a horror story or a fantasy epic, your muse may just as easily be a demon or a banshee, a dragon or a unicorn. Only you will know how you see her.

What you need
A statue or picture of your muse, a candle and a suitable holder

What you do

✪   Place the candle and the representation of your muse on your desk. Light the candle and call your muse by saying the following charm three times:

> *I call my muse through time and space*
> *To settle here within this place.*

- ✪ Wait until a sense of calm descends upon you. This is the arrival of your muse, the creative energy that you have called. Now settle down to your work. Remember to thank the muse and blow out the candle when your work is complete.
- ✪ Repeat this spell every time you start work.

Spell to aid concentration

Witches use crystals for a wide variety of purposes, tapping into their powers and harnessing their energies to our magic. Citrine, used in this spell, is a crystal of clarity and can help you to maintain focus and improve your powers of concentration. You can enhance this spell by performing it at midnight on a full moon.

What you need
5 citrine crystals, your pentacle

What you do
- ✪ Take the crystals and pentacle to your desk. Place the pentacle right in the middle and put the crystals on the pentacle to charge, as you do so, saying:

    I charge these crystals with the powers of focus, clarity and deep concentration. So be it!

    Leave the pentacle and crystals in place for 24 hours
- ✪ Holding one of the citrine crystals in your hand as you work, place the others one at each corner of your desk. The crystal in your hand will serve as a magnet, pulling the powers of the other four crystals towards you. The spell is complete. You should now find that you make great progress with your work.
- ✪ Recharge the crystals regularly by repeating the spell – once every three months should be sufficient unless you spend lots of time at your desk (for example, you are a full-time writer or home-worker), in which case you should re-charge the crystals monthly on the full moon.

Spell to help you meet deadlines

We all have deadlines of some sort, be they paying a bill, filing your accounts, completing an article or handing in an essay. I have found that it helps to set your own smaller deadlines too. For instance, if you have six months to write a thesis or complete a project, give yourself three months to complete the first draught, and a further two months for revision, editing and presentation. This way you will have your work completed one month ahead of the deadline and won't have any last-minute worries. In addition, try this spell.

What you need
A white candle with a suitable holder and your athame (or another inscribing tool); alternatively, a good supply of tea-lights and a single tea-light holder

What you do

⭐ Calculate how much work you have to do in how much time. For example, you may need to write 3,000 words in three days. This will give you an idea of how much work you need to do each day. By breaking up the job into smaller sections, you will find the task less daunting and your work will probably be of a higher standard – because you will not be rushing through it in a panic to get it done.

⭐ If you are using a candle, mark it up into the number of sections the task requires with your athame or inscribing tool.

⭐ Each day, allow the candle to burn down one section as you work, or allow one of the tea-lights to burn down entirely. When the entire candle or all the tea-lights has burnt down, you will have reached your deadline.

Spell to encourage creativity

To enhance this spell, perform it in conjunction with the Spell to Call Your Muse on pages 132–3.

What you need
An oil-burner fashioned to look like a faerie, your favourite oil

What you do

✪ Hold your hands, palms down, over the oil-burner and empower it with the following charm:

Faerie of creativity,
I call your powers here to me.
Fill my mind with visions strong;
Let me work the whole day long.
Help me to perfect my art;
Here is where my dreams will start.
Let the words/notes/images come swift and true.
Sacred being, inspire me, do!

✪ Use the burner to burn your favourite oil as you work. Each time you light the tea-light, repeat the charm once more.

Book divination

This is a great form of divination, and because it's so discreet, you can do it in a public library or book store just as easily as in a book-lined home study. You can use this process as often as you like. You might like to try using a friend's book collection.

What you do

- ⭐ Go to your bookshelves or into a bookshop or library, as you do so, concentrating on your question or dilemma. If you have nothing specific in mind, simply ask for general guidance. If you are in a bookshop or library, go to the section most relevant to your question – so if your question relates to love, you go to the relationships section; if your question relates to a holiday, you go to the travel section. If you are looking for general guidance or are not sure which section is most appropriate, go to the mind, body and spirit section, where all the magical books are usually kept.

- ⭐ Wander around the bookshelves, scanning them and focusing on your dilemma. You will eventually feel drawn to a particular shelf: the book that contains your answer is somewhere here. Run your finger along the spines of the books with your eyes closed and when it feels right, stop and take the book down.

- ⭐ Keep your eyes closed and open the book at random. Now open your eyes and read what you see on the page before you. It should shed some light on your current situation and may even give a very clear and specific answer to your question. You may now look at the title and flick through the rest of the book. If you're in a bookshop, you may even want to buy the book and read through the rest of its wisdom.

 A STUDY OF MAGIC

Spell for success in a creative venture

I'm sure that some of you out there have ambitions to work within the creative arts. Whether your goal is to be a top musician, a Hollywood actor, a great painter, an international author or a ballerina, a little magic can help to send you on your way – and can ease the hurt and frustration of disappointment. The road to success often entails facing rejection and criticism, and sometimes even accusations of laziness and impossible dreaming! The latter is especially likely to be the case if you have only a part-time day job so that you can concentrate on your main career goal. People may try to bully you into full-time employment or tell you to 'take your head out the clouds and get a real job'. The key is to remain focused on your ambition and know that persistence is crucial to success. And when you have achieved your dream and are replying to your fan mail, everyone will know why you spent ten years working part-time as a waitress. Remember, you have to believe in yourself before anyone else will!

What you need
A symbol of what you hope to achieve (for example, a paintbrush for an artist, a pointe shoe for a dancer and so on), your pentacle

What you do

✪ Place your symbol on your pentacle, on your desk or altar. Hold your hands over it, palms down, and say:

> *I empower this — as a symbol of my dreams. I will become a*
> *success and I will work hard to achieve that goal.*
> *This symbol is the seed of my ultimate dream and it will*
> *magnetise success to me.*
> *As I do will it, so shall it be!*

✪ The spell is complete. Keep your magical symbol with you while you work and as you attend auditions and so on. Re-empower it every full moon.

A spell to protect your Book of Shadows

As the most important book within the magical household, the Book of Shadows is usually protected by magic. If you are starting to create a book of your own, or have a one that you have been working on for a while, cast this spell to keep it safe from intrusive eyes. You will need two protective charms to do this magical working – preferably of silver, as this is the metal of the Goddess and witchcraft. You can get such charms from New age and occult shops. Good ones to choose are pentagrams, pentacles, crescent moons, Herne, Pan, moon witches, broomsticks and the triple moon symbol of the Goddess. You can pick different charms or two that are the same; it's up to you.

What you need
2 protective charms, a needle and thread, a length of red or black ribbon long enough to pass up the spine of your book and back down again (this will act as a page marker, so both ends of the ribbon should hang below the book), rosemary or basil essential oil

What you do
- ✪ Place the charms on your pentacle to charge for three days and nights.
- ✪ When the time is up, carefully sew the first charm onto one end of the ribbon, making sure it is secure and saying the following spell as you do so:

> *As I stitch and as I sew,*
> *I raise the power as I go.*
> *The magic of each little charm*
> *Keeps my Shadows safe from harm.*
> *From those who pry and those who peek,*
> *From prying eyes this Book they keep.*
> *As I will, it shall be so!*
> *I snip the thread and let the power go!*

- ✪ Repeat the spell as you sew on the second charm.

✪ Dab the lengths of ribbon with the rosemary or basil essential oil (both oils of protection). This will also give your magical book a delicious fragrance. Keep the ribbon inside your Book of Shadows.

Correspondences for the study

Oils and incenses	Crystals	Angels	Elementals	Power animals
Grapefruit	Clear quartz	Uriel	Sylph	Owl
Lemon balm	Citrine			Fox
Vanilla	Carnelian			
Basil				
Rosemary				

The Nursery and Children's Rooms

I t is important that children have a space they can call their own. This area will, of course, change as the child gets older and begins to have some input into the style of decor. To begin with, though, you will be responsible for creating the nursery. This should be a calm, quiet area where your baby can be soothed into restful sleep. It should also have space for all your baby's things.

The spells and rituals in this chapter will centre around the magical needs of babies, toddlers, children and teenagers – but first of all, a word about the magical nursery ...

The magical nursery

A theme of mythical creatures is a great idea for a magical nursery decor. Unicorns, faeries and mermaids are all good choices, as are friendly-looking dragons – think Puff rather than Draco! For a baby or toddler, add a couple of multi-faceted crystals to the window to fill the room with rainbows. Fairytales are another good source of inspiration. Most little girls will be thrilled with a princess-themed room. Look out for such decorative fairytale items as a glass slipper, a red cloak, a shiny red apple, a fancy mirror and so on. For a boy you could choose tales of bravery for your inspiration. Think about Robin Hood or the Knights of the Round Table and decorate accordingly, hanging wooden swords and shields on the walls, and, if you are artistic, designing heraldic flags and banners. If your children are older, they may enjoy helping with this.

Babies and toddlers

Having a new baby in the home is usually a joyful experience, but it is also often a very stressful one. Small babies depend on their parents to do everything for them and are therefore intensely demanding to care for. To keep things running as smoothly as possible, it is important that mother, father and baby get as much good-quality sleep as they possibly can. Of course, if the baby is sleeping soundly and regularly, the chances are that mum and dad will get a chance to rest too.

A bedtime routine will go a long way towards ensuring that even quite small babies get a good night's sleep. Look back at Chapter 8 for bedtime routine ideas – many of these can be adapted for babies and children. Giving your baby a warm bath prior to putting him or her down will almost certainly help, as will soft lighting and soothing sounds. CDs are available that simulate the sounds of the womb. These are said to calm even the most fretful of babies. If all else fails, try the following spell.

Spell for calm and restful sleep

What you do

✪ Follow your baby's usual bedtime routine. Then, before putting him down for the night, chant the following spell as you rock him:

> *Mother Goddess, bring your skill;*
> *Let my babe lie quiet and still.*
> *Let him/her sleep through the night,*
> *Until the first sign of Aurora's light.*
> *Mother of all, I summon thee;*
> *Let your mothering gifts flow through me.*

Spell to help you trust your own instincts

As a new mother you may find that well-meaning older women bombard you with advice. It may seem that to be considered a good mother, you must do everything the way your own mother or mother-in-law did them. But times change, and you are not your mother – it's okay to do things differently! The fact is that you and your child have the deepest connection there is. Whether you feel it right now or not is irrelevant; it is there nonetheless. All you need to do is trust your own instincts and go with the flow of natural motherhood magic!

What you do

⭐ When you feel in need of guidance, stop for a moment and speak the following chant:

> *Guiding spirits, hear my plea;*
> *Help me trust the feelings deep in me,*
> *To trust my instincts and go with the flow.*
> *As I will, it shall be so!*

Spell to help both parents bond with a new baby

While much is written about the bonding of mother and child, very little is said with regard to paternal bonding and the general strengthening of the family unit. This spell is designed to help father as well as mother feel included within this new phase of life.

What you do

⭐ As your baby sleeps in his cot, stand on one side, with the father on the other. One or both of you speak the following charm three times:

> *As one plus one did equal two,*
> *So two became one and we made you.*
> *Mother, father, baby bond,*
> *Make this family unit strong.*
> *Our magic now lies in the power of three,*
> *So seal this family. Let it be!*

Spell to enchant a teddy bear

Teddy bears and cuddly toys are popular gifts for newborns and children, and some of us keep our favourite childhood teddy well into adulthood, illustrating that this is a very important purchase! Pick a toy that is well made and will stand the test of time. It should be strong enough to survive the tantrums of a toddler. Bear in mind the magical associations of colour as you make your choice (consult the tables of correspondences at the end of each chapter for more information).

What you need
A carefully chosen new teddy bear, your pentacle, some lavender essential oil

What you do

✪ Once you have your teddy bear, wait for the next full moon. On this night, take all you need to your altar. Lay the teddy on your pentacle, on your altar, and light the altar candles.

✪ Splash the teddy with a few drops of the lavender essential oil. Then hold your hands, palms down, over the teddy and chant the following chant, continuing for as long as you can remain focused:

> *When Mum and Dad cannot be there,*
> *Our love is felt through this bear.*

✪ When you have finished, blow out the candles and give the newly enchanted teddy to your child.

Spell to keep a toddler safe

As babies begin to crawl and then toddle, they can get themselves into all kinds of scrapes. Every home is full of hidden dangers, so when your baby gets mobile, the first thing you need to do is baby-proof your house! Make sure there are no electrical leads or wires, pan handles or sharp objects within your child's reach. Lock away all detergents, medicines, paints and so on, and fit baby-gates to staircases. Once your home is as safe an environment as you can make it, try this spell.

What you do

⭐ Pop the child on your knee and, while giving him a cuddle, say the following protection rite – if your child is in a more exuberant mood, you could turn the rhyme into a clapping or bouncing game:

> *Little child, into all you see,*
> *Let no harm come to thee.*
> *Walking, talking, toddling free,*
> *By Mother's love, protected be!*

⭐ Repeat the rite daily to be on the safe side!

School days

As young children begin to grow up, they are faced with the challenges of playgroup, nursery and, of course, school. This time when they must leave the safety of home and learn how to interact with a room full of strangers can be a frightening one for them. For mothers, releasing their child into the big wide world can be a huge wrench, too. For a time, what teacher says may become more important than what Mummy says, and it can be difficult to accept that other people will now have an influence over your child.

Reassurance is the key word at this stage. Your child needs to know that you are always there for them – and, as a parent, you have to learn to trust that your child will always come back. Examples of this classic little drama can be seen on any visit to the park or playground. Children bounce off to the swings or the slide, while Mum sits watching on a park bench – but periodically, they will run back to Mum, for no apparent reason, and then trot off again. I can clearly remember doing this myself as a small child. I didn't want my mother for anything really; I simply needed to know that she was still where I had left her! Sometimes children just need to touch base in this way.

Spell to welcome the wider world

What you need

A recent photo of your child

What you do

⭐ Take the photo of your child to your altar. Light the candles and place the photo in front of you on the altar. Sit for a while and think of all that you and your child have been through and accomplished together – his first steps, first word and so on were as much your triumph as his.

⭐ Now focus strongly on your child remaining happy, healthy and safe as he begins to venture forth into the world of school.

⭐ Maintaining this visualisation, repeat the following charm three times (changing the pronouns to reflect the sex of your child):

As the tide of life carries forth this child,
I prepare to step aside.
As life shapes and moulds and nurtures him,
I trust that he'll enjoy the ride.
As my love enfolds him all the while,
Keeping him from harm,
His adventures only make him smile;
His life is filled with calm.
As he returns to me every day
To tell me all he knows,
First in his heart I know I'll stay,
Protecting him from woes.
So mote it be!

⭐ Blow out the candles and go about your day.

Teenagers

Teenagers are notoriously difficult to handle, probably because they have so much going on in their lives, their bodies and their minds. Setting boundaries and imposing curfews will help to maintain a sense of control and fair discipline, while entrusting your teenager with his freedom once in a while can help to encourage good behaviour in the long term. You should also respect teenagers' need for privacy with regard to their own room.

One of the biggest complaints against teenagers is that they never tidy their rooms. One way to encourage tidiness is to provide a trendy space with lots and lots of storage! Then try working the following spell.

Spell for a tidy room

What you need
A clear quartz crystal

What you do

 Take the clear quartz crystal and walk three times deosil (clockwise) around your teen's room, as you do so, saying:

> *Powers of the crystal and powers that be,*
> *Make him/her tidy this room! So mote it be!*

 Cleanse the crystal by running it under the cold tap, as it will have absorbed any negativity present in the room. Repeat the spell as often as necessary!

Flying the nest

Eventually your children will grow up and leave home. This can be a heart-wrenching and lonely time for some parents; however, it is part of the natural process of life. Independence is, after all, what we bring up our children for. While it's a good idea to leave your child's room as it is for a while, in case they need to return home, this should not be a long-term arrangement. Give your child a year to 18 months to settle down away from home, and then set about turning their room into something new – perhaps a place where you can indulge in your favourite hobby.

You could, for example, convert a former bedroom into a home gym, with all your exercise equipment set up. It could become a study, where you can finally begin to write that novel; a sewing room; an artist's studio; or an altar room for magic. Embrace this new phase of life and welcome your freedom. Be there when your children need you, but remember that you are more than just a mother.

Correspondences for the nursery and children's rooms

Oils and incenses	Crystals	Angels	Elementals	Power animals
Lavender	Faceted rainbow crystals	Gabriel	Undine	Bear
Vanilla	Amethyst	Michael	Sylph	Unicorn
Patchouli			Pixie	
Jasmine			Elf	
Frankincense				

A Spell in the Garden

The garden is a truly sacred space, as this is where we commune with the powers of earth and sky. Observing the passing seasons and the endless cycle of birth, death and rebirth is a fundamental part of witchcraft. To witches, connecting with nature is a way of attuning with the goddess and god of Wiccan belief. If you have a garden attached to your home, begin to regard this as your piece of sacred land, a place where you feel the great heartbeat of Mother Earth and can call on these powers in your magic.

At one time, a garden was an essential means of survival, and even the poorest little cottage would have a small patch of earth producing potatoes, turnips, carrots and so on. Still today, with vegetables readily available in prepared and packaged forms, many people choose to grow their own produce, filling their gardens with runner beans, strawberries and greenhouses full of tomatoes. My own garden yields a bountiful crop of blackberries and elderberries year after year, and my best friend's mother is understandably proud of her home-grown strawberries. Most of us know where an apple tree grows, and schoolchildren still indulge in the forbidden practice of 'scrumping'!

Gardens are also a source of great beauty. Their flowers wave and nod at us as we pass by, delighting us with their vibrant colours and heady scents. Roses are an old English favourite, closely followed in the popularity stakes by tulips, daffodils, harebells, delphiniums and crocuses. The wild flower garden is a personal favourite of mine, as I love bluebells, foxgloves, buttercups and so on. Some clever cooks couldn't imagine life without their herb garden, where they grow their own delicate flavours to season their culinary masterpieces. Herbs are also a staple of the witch's garden, along with sacred trees such as hawthorn, elder, ash, oak and holly.

Even if your fingers aren't that green, you can still create a beautiful garden by using the right combination of outdoor furniture, pots, statues and garden ornaments. Creating any sort of garden is hard work and time-consuming in the short term, but in the long term you will have a sacred space that is ever changing and growing, that attracts wildlife and provides a source of great relaxation and endless beauty. Even the balcony of a high-rise flat can be filled with pots, tubs and windowboxes containing herbs, flowers and small shrubs. Add a folding chair and a bird table and you have created a beautiful sacred space.

From a magical point of view, there are many possibilities for creating a garden, including herb gardens, secret gardens with hidden altars, faerie gardens and wildlife gardens. Ask yourself what kind of garden your soul craves. A faerie garden is perfect if you have small children, while a secret garden is more suitable if you like to work outdoors but are overlooked by a neighbour. If you have a large garden, perhaps you could divide it into various zones: a dark corner beneath tall trees could be your secret garden, a series of pots by the kitchen window or back door could be a herb garden, a play area for the kids could be combined with a faerie dell, and a secluded arbour or summerhouse could be covered in roses to make a quiet space for reading, contemplation and meditation. If you love the sound of rustling wheat fields but live in the city, plant tall grasses that will rustle in the same way. If you are keen on wildlife, think about including birdtables, bat boxes, hedgehog homes and so on, and put food out each evening for any creatures that may want it. You may find, as I did, that a fox begins to visit regularly, or a family of badgers, like the ones who visit my brother's garden each night. Let your imagination run as wild as a meadow!

Some homes have transitional spaces attached to them in the form of a conservatory. A conservatory makes a fabulous altar room, in which you are close to nature whatever the weather. You can work all your magic here if you wish, enjoying the comfort of indoors while drawing on the powers of outdoors. A garden shed, chalet or summerhouse can serve the same purpose.

But before any magic can take place, you will need to make a connection with the land on which you live. Remember that the land deva can help you with this (see pages 37–40), so attune with her regularly, expressing your wish for a beautiful garden that is filled with magic. You may even find that you experience a shot of inspiration and come up with great new ideas. This is the land deva communicating with you, telling you what the land needs and what type of garden would please and suit the energies of its elementals. If you perform the land deva spells in Chapter 3, you will receive not only the inspiration for a magical garden but also the means to put your ideas into practice and manifest the garden of your dreams!

Spell to feel the great heart beat

Just as people and animals have a heartbeat, so too does the land. The pulse of the earth is not exactly audible but it can certainly be felt if you lie still on the ground for a few moments and open yourself to it. This is a great exercise for those occasions when you're feeling overwhelmed by a particular challenge or when you need an additional source of power to help you through a tough time. It can also usefully be carried out prior to working any magic that calls upon the elemental powers of earth – prosperity spells, for example, will be greatly enhanced if you attune with the heartbeat of the land just before you start to work.

What you do

- ✪ Lie on the ground, face down with your ear to the earth, and stay there quietly for a few moments, absorbing the natural energies surrounding you.
- ✪ Now imagine drawing up a deep-green light from the earth into your own heart. This mental connection will help you to connect with the heartbeat of the earth beneath you. You will know that you have made this connection when you feel grounded and relaxed.
- ✪ Now focus on pulling the earth's strength into yourself. You are connected with the heartbeat of the earth.

  A SPELL IN THE GARDEN

The magical herb garden

Most witches and magical practitioners make use of herbs in their spells. Often these are bought ready dried, but some witches prefer to grow, harvest and dry their own herbs specifically for use in magic. This has its advantages. You can plant and harvest in accordance with the cycle of the moon, thus adding lunar magic to the powers of the herbs themselves. You can also place appropriate stones and crystals at the foot of each herb to increase its power – for example, an aventurine crystal placed next to a mint plant will draw in the powers of prosperity, while a piece of rose quartz at the foot of a rosemary plant will attract love.

Herbs are generally quite hardy, requiring little other than watering, so don't be put off growing them if you don't have green fingers. Because witches tend to grow fond of their magical herb gardens, it's a good idea to plant in tubs and containers; then, should you ever move house, you can take your herb garden with you. When creating a magical herb garden, you should plant at the new moon, when the universal energies are conducive to growth and expansion. Always harvest your herbs at the full moon, as this is the most powerful time magically. The only exception to this rule is when you are harvesting a herb for banishing or binding spells, in which case you should cut it during the waning moon. No herbs should ever be cut during the dark moon, as this is a period of rest and the magical energies of your herbs will be at their weakest.

If herb gardening interests you, good herbs to begin with are:

- ✪ Mint for prosperity
- ✪ Rosemary for love
- ✪ Basil for empowerment
- ✪ Lavender for healing and dream magic
- ✪ Mugwort for psychic abilities
- ✪ Catnip for a feline familiar
- ✪ Marjoram for happiness
- ✪ Vetivert and thistle for protection

A standard range of herbs such as this will form the basis of your magical herb garden, and you can add to it over time, introducing new herbs as you learn more about them and as individual spells call for them. When you harvest your herbs, remember to cut gently with a sharp knife. You should never hack away at these delicate forms of life. Before cutting, most witches silently ask the plant deva:

> *May I have permission to take from this plant for*
> *the purpose of magic?*

Wait a few moments and, if all seems well, go ahead and make your cut. If you begin to feel nervous or uneasy, however, this is a sign that the deva has refused permission, perhaps due to the plant's state of health or growth. Pick a different plant and ask again – or use a dried version.

To dry your own herbs

Once you have a collection of herbs, both fresh and dried, you will be able to make powerful magic using these gifts of the earth.

What you need
A bunch of your chosen herb, a mortar and pestle, an airtight jar, a label

What you do

- ⭐ Hang the bunch of herbs upside down in a cool, dry place. It will take time for them to dry properly (how much time depends on the individual herb), so be patient. As a rule of thumb, the longer you leave them to dry, the better. If the herbs are not absolutely dry, they will go mouldy in the jar and will be useless.
- ⭐ Once the herbs are completely dry, un-bunch them and grind them in a deosil (clockwise) direction using the mortar and pestle.
- ⭐ Place the ground herbs in the airtight container and label it accordingly.

A SPELL IN THE GARDEN

A quiet place

A garden is a fabulous place to take time out for quiet contemplation or meditation. If you do plan to meditate outdoors, you will need to create a quiet space in which to do so. You may find that you already have items of garden furniture that could be used for this purpose, or you might choose to buy something new. A summerhouse can make a fantastic garden temple. Keep inside it a few well chosen items to represent your personal idea of divinity and the sacred art of magic. A small arbour could become your personal 'thinking spot' – simply place a bench beneath a shady tree, hedge or rose-covered trellis and sit and mull things over. A traditional garden hammock is great for meditations and astral travel. These days you don't even need trees in your garden to sling up a hammock; you can buy them complete with their own supporting frame. With just a little thought and effort, and without too much expense or inconvenience, you can create a quiet, peaceful retreat in your garden – a place where you can relax, meditate, visualise or just while away a pleasant afternoon.

Winds of change

Every witch's cottage has a weather vane. Weather vanes are making a welcome come-back and can be bought from garden centres for as little as £50. They are made in a wide range of styles, including faeries and dragons. But perhaps the most appropriate weather vane for a magical household is fashioned to look like a witch flying on her broomstick or bending over a simmering cauldron. A black cat weather vane would also be in keeping with the magical home, and is slightly more discreet – people will just think you like cats!

Erect your weather vane somewhere high and exposed to the elements, making sure that you attach it securely, and use its guidance in your magic. For example, a west wind generally brings rain, so when the wind is coming from this direction, you could request that cleansing and healing energies be sent to someone who needs them. A north wind is associated with the powers of Earth, so prosperity and growth spells will be greatly enhanced when the wind blows from this direction. East winds bring clarity and wisdom, and south winds love, passion and protection. For weather witching, call up a north wind for frosts and snows in winter, an east wind for a gentle breeze, a south wind for a warm sunny day, and a west wind for rains and storms. An easy way to call the winds is to stand facing the appropriate direction and say:

> *Wind of the — (state direction) I call to thee;*
> *Bring here your gifts; I summon thee!*

Alternatively, focus on the type of weather required and whistle into that direction (or play a wind instrument such as a recorder). This is known as whistling in the wind.

Stone circle

All over the British Isles are the remains of ancient stone circles. The most famous is, of course, Stonehenge, closely followed by the circle at Avebury in Wiltshire and the circle of Callanish on the Isle of Lewis, off the Scottish coast. Such circles as these have a strong aura of magic and power. While we may only guess at their original purpose, it is easy to imagine that they could once have been the back-drop to some elaborate magical ceremony.

If you are lucky enough to have a relatively large garden, you could create your own stone circle. This could be a permanent feature or you could create it each time you work magic outdoors.

For a permanent stone circle you will probably need some help, so gather together all your friends and family members who are of a like mind. Work out how many stones you will need for the size of circle you require. Remember that the stones need not be very large – the magic lies in the symbolism and your intent. You can get stones from garden centres, and many have a delivery service, which will save you from damaging the suspension of your car! Once you have your stones, consecrate them by sprinkling them with a mixture of spring water and rock salt. As you do so say:

> *I bless this stone as a tool of my magic. May its earth powers*
> *help me to create a sacred space. So mote it be!*

Once you have consecrated all the stones, dig holes and place the stones upright within the earth to create your circle. A large flat stone laid in the centre could be used as an outdoor altar.

A temporary circle could be made using pebbles, rocks, or even crystals or sea shells. This should be taken up after your magical working, so if you are going to use this circle again, you will need a box to keep your stones in. While this version of the stone circle may not seem quite as romantic, it is just as powerful and has the added advantage that it can be taken with you if you move. Also, you need not stick to a simple circle but could use the stones to create spirals, pentagrams and so on, as the magic dictates. It is a more practical solution for a smaller garden or for those of you who have children and need to keep the lawn clear for them to play on most of the time. Remember to bless and consecrate the stones in the same way.

The wildlife altar

The garden is the perfect place to attune with wildlife and to set up an altar dedicated to the animals who live in and around your garden. Whenever we erect a bird table, we are attuning in this way on an entirely unconscious level. In magical households, however, we try to provide sustenance not just for the birds but for all creatures who need our assistance. This may mean having bird-feeders for the squirrels and anti-squirrel-feeders for the birds! In short, we try to make sure that there is something for everyone.

If you would like to create a wildlife altar, begin with a basic bird table, putting out bread, cheese, ham and bacon rind – the latter will help to replenish the vital fat reserves that keep animals alive through the winter. Fill feeders with nuts and seeds for both birds and squirrels, and put out fresh water every day.

Now turn your attention to the floor around the bird table. Here you should place a bowl of fresh water and a bowl of food for any land-loving animals who may visit your garden. Kitchen scraps and pet food can provide much needed sustenance for foxes, hedgehogs, badgers, and even stray cats and dogs. This is especially important during the winter months, when natural food sources are scarce and want is keenly felt.

In addition to the altar, install a bird bath and place a few nesting boxes for different types of animal in quiet corners of your garden. Homes for bats, birds, squirrels and hedgehogs can all be bought from garden centres, or you can make them yourself if you have the skill. This is a great way to bring the power of familiars to your magical home. Hang special cakes for birds and squirrels on trees and shrubs, and put out a little unsalted popcorn too – the smaller birds love it, and it's so light they can even carry it home with them!

Finally, once you begin feeding the wildlife, it is important that you don't stop – think how you would feel if the local supermarket closed down overnight and you were faced with having to find, grow and make your own food in order to survive. Not a pleasant thought, is it? Animals will come to know that they can always find a meal in your garden, and may reward you by nesting there or nearby as a result, so please don't disappoint them!

Wiccan garden altar

If you have a secluded spot in your garden, or you don't mind the neighbours knowing of your magical interests, you can set up a Wiccan garden altar to attune with the powers of nature. A sturdy table or bench will provide an altar surface. You can paint this or leave it to take on the weathered look that the elements will give it. Anything you place on this altar should be left outdoors, so save your best pewter chalice for your indoor altar. Many occult and New Age shops sell altar figures that are weather-proof, so you might like to invest in one of these. If finances are a problem, most garden centres sell wall plaques fashioned to look like Green Men or star, sun and moon faces. Any of these is appropriate to an outdoor altar, and they are relatively

inexpensive. An outdoor water feature could be placed near your garden altar so that you have the relaxing sound of water to work to.

A pentagram made up of fallen twigs would look great on a garden altar. You could make a few and hang them from nearby trees and hedges too. Perhaps the most important tool for an outdoor altar is an offering bowl. It is here that you will place your offerings, and occasionally a libation after a ritual, as a gift to the powers of the earth. A pottery pet bowl is ideal, as this will not be spoilt by bad weather. Remember to make your garden altar unique to yourself, and also bear in mind that an outdoor altar should be much simpler and more rugged than your indoor ones.

The faerie dell

The garden is the realm of the elementals and faerie folk, or the fey as they are also known. It is here that their powers can be most strongly felt, and they should always be acknowledged. There are various ways to do this, so choose the one that best suits you and your garden. A traditional way to honour the fey is to allow a corner of the garden to grow wild. Alternatively, you might like to create a small wild-flower garden. Planting foxgloves – the faerie flower – is a great way to invite and acknowledge the presence of the faerie folk. Or you could add statues of faeries and other elemental beings, such as dryads, to your garden. This will create a wonderfully magical effect – a garden perfect for children to play in, or just for those of you who have always loved faeries! Once you have created your faerie dell, try any of the spells and rituals below, all of which call on the powers of faeries and elementals.

To honour the dryad

Trees are beautiful, magical and essential to our existence. The elementals of trees are called dryads, and these magical beings preside over the health and growth of the particular tree that they are attached to. If you have trees in your garden, first of all be thankful, as they are helping to cleanse the air you breathe. Second, be respectful: they are probably far older than you are! Third, honour the dryad of the tree by performing this ritual. If you can, do this at the sabbat of Mabon (21 September), Samhain (31 October) or Yule (21 December). If this is not possible, work at the time of the full moon.

What you need

A saucepan, some cider, a little ground cinnamon, your cauldron, a wooden spoon, a ladle

What you do

- ⭐ Heat the cider in the saucepan, adding a sprinkling of ground cinnamon.
- ⭐ Once the cider has warmed through, transfer it to your cauldron and stir the liquid in a pentacle shape, using a wooden spoon.
- ⭐ Take the cauldron out to the trees in your garden. Moving around your garden in a deosil (clockwise) direction, stand at the foot of each tree in turn and pour three ladles of cider at the roots, as you do so, saying:

> *By the strength of the apple that fell from the tree,*
> *I honour you, dryad, and give nourishment to thee.*

The faerie triad

If you are planning to plant trees in your garden, why not plant the three trees of the faerie triad – oak, ash and thorn (or hawthorn)? Tradition states that where these three trees grow, the power of faerie magic is immense, and a door to the Otherworld lies waiting to be discovered!

To re-create the faerie triad in your own garden, imagine an equilateral triangle superimposed upon your planting space. Plant an oak tree at the apex of the triangle, an ash tree at the left-hand corner and a hawthorn tree at the right-hand corner. Honour the dryad of each tree with the ritual above and then perform the spell below on each new tree.

Spell to protect a tree

What you need
A black marker pen, your athame (or a tool for inscribing in the soil)

What you do

⭐ Using the marker pen, draw upon the trunk of the tree a circle with an equal armed cross within it. This is the ancient symbol of earth power and earth magic.

⭐ Use your athame (or other tool) to draw a circle in the ground all around the trunk of the tree. If this isn't possible for any reason, draw a pentagram in the earth in front of the tree instead.

⭐ Lay your hands on the tree trunk and repeat the following charm three times:

> *Sacred plant of strength and growth,*
> *Standing people of the North,*
> *With branches wide and leaves so green,*
> *Be protected from harm, seen and unseen!*
> *Standing tall and standing strong,*
> *Sacred plant of life so long,*
> *With Craft and spell I honour thee.*
> *Grow for me! So mote it be!*

Spell for growth

This simple ritual will help your garden to grow. Perform it every full moon, throughout the seasons of spring and summer. It is important to work with the cycles of nature, so do not use this spell in autumn or winter, which are the seasons of rest and decay. Growth magic can be begun at Imbolc (2 February).

What you do

✪ At the witching hour, walk all around the perimeter of your garden three times. As you do so, visualise your garden growing better than it ever has before, producing bigger and more beautiful blooms; tastier fruit and vegetables; stronger, taller trees; thicker hedges and so on. As you walk, chant the following charm:

> *Grow, grow, I bid you grow!*

Spell to enchant a faerie statue

If you have a special statue of a faerie or angel in your garden, you can enchant it with the powers of nature. This spell can be repeated with as many statues as you like. It's a good idea to have at least four – one for each cardinal point of your garden.

What you do

✪ First of all, give the faerie a name, as this will help you to connect with the magical powers it represents.

✪ Go to each of the four directions, lifting the statue high into the air at each one and asking for the blessings of the element by saying:

> *I ask for the blessings of — and call elemental powers into this statue. So be it!*

✪ Place the statue in your chosen spot and pour a little milk over it to connect this new tool with the powers of life. The magical energies of this now enchanted statue will protect and enhance your magical garden.

A SPELL IN THE GARDEN

Gateway of the holly king

The holly king is an aspect of the Green Man, the masculine spirit of nature, and he can provide powerful protection and guardianship if called on. You can invoke his strength and assistance by placing holly plants outside the entrance of your property – for instance, a couple of miniature holly trees in tubs at either side of your front door. This is an ideal arrangement if you live in a flat and your magical garden is situated on a small balcony.

If your garden is large enough, however, try planting a holly bush at either side of your garden gate. Once the bush is planted, water it with a good plant food solution and say the following charm three times:

> *Holly king of prickled leaf,*
> *Protect me and mine from harm and grief;*
> *Guard my property from every foe,*
> *Or your retribution they shall know!*

Elder magic

The elder tree is sacred to the witches' goddess in her aspect of Crone. As a result, the elder has come to be associated with the stereotypical witch – the old, bent hag of folklore and fairytale. But witches know that there is another side to the Crone, one of wisdom, teaching and protection. It is the Crone who knows the deepest mysteries of magic and spell, of birth, death and rebirth, and all the realms in between. If you have an elder growing in your garden, respect this tree most of all. Do not cut it down, uproot it or do any other harm to this tree, as to do so is to bring about a run of bad luck. The magical energies of the elder are very powerful and can best be attuned with on the sabbat of Samhain, known to non-witches as Halloween.

To attune with an elder tree

Perform this ritual on Samain (31 October).

What you need
A chalice of elderberry wine or elderberry juice

What you do
⭐ Just after dusk has fallen, go to the elder tree, taking with you the chalice of wine or juice. Stand before the tree and sip a little of the wine, then tap the chalice three times on the trunk of the tree and empty the contents at its foot. Now say:

> Elder tree, I see through thee
> To the Crone behind.
> As darkness fell, I cast this spell
> My own wisdom now to find.
> Guide me on this path I take,
> As my courage I do summon;
> Foolishness I now forsake
> To be replaced with the wisdom of woman.

Magical pest control

If you have a pest problem in your garden, rather than using pesticides, try this simple spell, repeating it daily until the creatures responsible get the message! Although you should not expect instant results, you may be surprised at just how quickly this technique works.

What you do
⭐ Go out into your garden, settle down in a comfortable spot and allow your mind to become quiet.
⭐ Close your eyes and bring to mind the image of the insect or other creature you're having problems with. Strongly visualise this creature and all its kind leaving your garden and moving elsewhere. Keep up the visualisation for as long as your focus is clear.

Creating a faerie ring

Just as we can make our own stone circle, we can also create a faerie ring within our garden. The way you go about this will depend on the type of circle you want. If you would like to create a living faerie ring, then buy lots of wild flower seeds and plant these close together in a perfect circle. Of course, this form of circle requires that you have the patience to wait until the flowers grow and is obviously not suitable for urgent magical workings!

A more decorative and instantaneous faerie ring can be created by making a circle of mushroom, toadstool and dancing faerie sculptures. This kind of circle is ideal if you have children and would like to introduce them to the elementals; a relationship with the faeries can persuade younger children to take care of their environment. An advantage of this type of circle is that, if need be, you can pack it away when it is not in use or take it with you when you move house.

Choose whichever method suits you best and use the faerie ring as a magic circle in which to cast your spells.

Correspondences for the garden

Oils and incenses	Crystals	Angels	Elementals	Power animals
Citronella	All natural rocks, stones, pebbles, etc.	Uriel	Gnome	Bird
			Sylph	Insect
			Elf	Hedgehog
				Squirrel
				Mole

Moving Home

Moving home is one of the most stressful things you can do to yourself – statistics state that it's right up there with getting divorced and suffering a bereavement! If you own your own home and are part of a buyers' chain, you will probably have to deal with disappointments and let-downs. If you rent, you will probably be faced with viewing, accepting and moving into a property within a very short space of time, sometimes as little as seven days. Each scenario brings about its own particular challenges. In this chapter we will be looking at some of these challenges and exploring magical ways to overcome them. We will also be looking at some of the many magical ways to manifest your very own dream home in your personal reality.

Moving home is a new beginning, a fresh start. As such, it is a time of excitement and anticipation. It is also a time when we tend to have one foot in the past and one in the future, and this can lead to feelings of turmoil, confusion and a general state of imbalance. It is important that we do all we can to restore equilibrium as soon as possible and that we take the stress factor into account in our communications with family and friends.

Usually we move house because we want to. Leaving home for the first time, upgrading to a bigger or better property, or relocating to a nicer area are all very positive reasons for a house move. At other times, however, circumstances beyond our control force us to leave our home and begin again elsewhere. This form of uprooting can be a devastating and traumatic experience, and may leave us feeling very much at odds with our new environment. Finding a sense of belonging can then be difficult, especially if you have had to move many times. Eventually, however, your natural nesting instinct will take over if you let it, and you will slowly begin to root yourself in your new life – albeit quite superficially at first. None of us develops a sense of belonging overnight, so give yourself time to adapt and settle in.

There are occasions, too, when we're not sure if a house move is really the right thing. This may be the case if you are moving to get away from something. If you are dealing with racism, prejudice or domestic violence, a move may be the only way to put an end to a negative situation. However, if you are moving to avoid an issue that needs to be dealt with, consider whether you might be running away. No matter how tempting running away may seem, it usually doesn't work. At some point in your life, you will be forced to deal with the issue you are fleeing. In this situation, it might be better to stick things out and wait for the dust to settle.

But what if it's simply a question of indecision? Well, magic can help you to make up your mind. I'm a huge fan of pros and cons lists: they help to clarify the overall situation and can highlight any fears you may have. Whatever your house-move dilemma, make a list of all the reasons for and against, and you will find arriving at a decision much easier. Once all the factors in a situation are there in front of you in black and white, it's far more difficult to hide from the truth!

You could also try dowsing for an insight into your current situation – try the following divination.

Should I move house divination

What you need
A pendulum (these are available from occult and New Age shops, but you can make your own by tying a heavy object – a key is ideal – to a piece of string)

What you do
✪ Sit on the floor of your home to ground yourself and quiet your mind.

✪ Breathe deeply for a few moments, then take up your pendulum, holding it lightly but firmly. First of all, ask a yes/no question to which you know the answer. Note which way your pendulum swings for yes and which way for no. You are now ready to begin your divination.

✪ Work through the following questions (or ones of your own choosing), making a note of the answers.
  * Do I truly wish to move house?
  * Is a move for my highest good and for the highest good of my family?
  * Will the problems I am experiencing end with a house move?
  * If I stay here, will my problems be resolved in time?
  * Will a move enhance my relationships?
  * Will a move affect my employment? For better? For worse?
  * Will I find the house of my dreams?
  * Have I already seen my new home?
  * Will I settle down easily in my new home? Will my family?
  * Will the move go well?
  * Should I move home in the near future?

✪ Study your list of answers to these basic questions and consider your decision.

House hunting

House hunting can be almost as stressful as the move itself! This is usually because we have only a very general idea of what we want. The house-buying experts tell us to leave our options open, prepare to compromise and so on. In magic, however, the foundation of all workings is to ask for exactly what you want and be specific! So what if you apply this magical law to house hunting?

First of all, you must decide what you want. I realise this sounds like simple common sense, but it's surprising how many people wander through life with only a vague idea of where they might like to end up! Don't let yourself be like that, especially when it comes to something as important as your home. Remember how specific you were in your Dream Home book (see pages 28–40)? Well, this is how detailed you must be every time you move house on the way to your dream home.

Spell to manifest the home you desire

What you need
A pen and some paper, a white candle, your cauldron

What you do
- ✪ Take the pen and paper and write down exactly what you want from your next home.
- ✪ Copy what you have written onto a new piece (or pieces) of paper and roll the second list into a scroll.
- ✪ Light the candle and (using the first list) read aloud what you have written.
- ✪ Set light to the scroll of paper in the candle and put it into your cauldron to burn down, as you do so, saying:

> *Goddess of manifestation,*
> *Mother of all my dreams,*
> *Please manifest what I've written here.*
> *So mote it be!*

- ✪ Place the first list somewhere you can see it every day.

To connect with your chosen property

So you have found a house you that looks promising and you are going to view it in a few days. A great way to ensure the house becomes yours is to connect with it magically.

What you need
A picture of your chosen property (from the estate agent's brochure or property guide) or the full address of the property on a slip of paper, an envelope

What you do
- ✪ When you go to view the property, pick up something from the place itself – for example, a leaf from the hedge or a paint peeling. Keep this safe and take it home with you.

⭐ Once you are home, place the picture or slip of paper with the address of your chosen property in the envelope. Add the leaf or whatever you picked up from the property and seal the envelope. Carry this with you at all times, keeping it as close to your skin as you can. At night sleep with it under your pillow. You should begin to feel your connection to the house deepen – you may begin to dream of the property or think about it constantly during the day. When this happens, push the sale forward and try working the following spell.

Spell to avoid being gazumped

What you do

⭐ Repeat the following chant every day, as many times as you can, as you do so, holding a clear image of your chosen property in your mind:

Gazumped I command I shall not be;
By magic and spell, so shall it be!

⭐ Keep up the chanting – at least every morning and evening – until you know for certain that the property is yours and you are ready to move in.

Spell to push the deal through quickly

To make sure things don't stagnate, work this spell to push the final deal through quickly, easily and without a hitch.

What you need
A large white candle, your athame or an inscribing tool, a little sunflower oil, some dried basil

What you do
- ⭐ Using your athame or the inscribing tool, inscribe upon the candle the address of the property you're buying and the price you're willing to pay.
- ⭐ Anoint the candle with the sunflower oil (for success) and roll it in the dried basil (a magical rocket fuel that makes anything go with a bang!).
- ⭐ Light the candle and sit before it, chanting the following charm:

    Push through the deal and let it flow;
    As I will, it shall be so!

- ⭐ Continue chanting for as long as you remain focused, then blow out the candle.
- ⭐ Repeat this process on a daily basis until the deal is signed and sealed. Use more candles if necessary. Once the deal has gone through, on your first night in your new house, burn the remains of the candle and bury them in the garden of your new property

Moving out

We now come to the most stressful part of all – the big move! Sorting out and packing up are the order of the day – usually made even more difficult by friendly neighbours coming in to wish you well, excited pets and confused children who insist on unpacking all their toys just to make sure nothing has been forgotten! It may be difficult to keep your cool amidst all this turmoil, but that it exactly what you have to do. If you need a few moments to de-stress and gather your thoughts, not to mention your second wind, go for a walk or have a quick shower or bath to relax and refresh you. On your return to work, try to go about things in a methodical manner, doing what needs to be done and delegating where possible.

Making lists can be a big help, even if it is just for the satisfaction of being able to tick things off as you work! In this way you can see that you are actually making progress, although it may not feel that way as you look around the house. A list will also remind you to do all those important things like cancelling the milk and hiring the removal van! If you do make a list, pin it on a wall or door and leave it there, with a pen nearby, as there is nothing more frustrating than losing your 'things to do' list when you have a million things to do!

Moving folklore

Like other aspects of household life, moving has its own collection of folk beliefs. The best day to move is generally thought to be a Sunday, bringing abundance and prosperity to all involved. Moving on a Friday is said to bring love and passion. Friday is the day of Venus/Aphrodite, goddess of love and beauty, so a newly wed couple would do well to move into their marital home on this day. The most magical day to move is Monday, the day of the moon. Choose this day if you are Wiccan or a magical practitioner, as it will bring luck and blessings to your spellcraft and will enchant your home with magic. A Tuesday move will bring about closer family bonds, a Wednesday move will sharpen the psychic powers of those living in the new house, and a Thursday move will bring better career prospects and is great for those who work from home. Moving on a Saturday is generally thought to be bad luck, as this day is ruled by Saturn, god of melancholy and darkness. However, if your move is intended to banish a negative life pattern such as domestic violence, then Saturday is the best day to pluck up your courage and go for it.

Moving on a sunny day is said to bring good fortune and happiness, while rain and clouds are darker omens and may spell trouble for a time. A flurry of snow as you move means that you are protected by angels, and your new home will be full of peace and joy.

The phases of the moon play a role in the folklore of moving. To move house on the new moon is to make a fresh start, while to move on the full moon brings luck and blessings. Move on a waning moon if you wish to banish unhappiness experienced in the old home. The dark moon is most suitable if you need to do a 'moonlight flit' and also if you are fleeing from abuse or prejudice, as the dark goddess associated with this moon will protect and guide you.

Ritual to find the best removal firm

When it comes to moving all your treasured possessions from one place to another, you need a removal company that you can trust. Let's face it, you've put your whole life in a series of boxes and you want it all to arrive safely at your chosen destination. There are some cowboy firms out there who will use your grandmother's antique china for their many tea-breaks, breaking the china in the process! Instead of just opting for the first company you happen to come across, use a little magic and be guided to a removal team that will treat your things with due care and respect.

What you need
A copy of the Yellow Pages

What you do
- ✪ Place the Yellow Pages on your knee and lay your hands on top of it, palms down.

⭐ Close your eyes and say:

> *May I be guided to a removal firm that I can trust, one that will take good care of my belongings and will deliver them safely and efficiently to my new home. May they be polite, respectful and easy to get on with, making my house move a pleasant, stress-free experience. This is my will. May my hands and eyes be guided by magic. So be it!*

⭐ Open your eyes and find the removals section of the Yellow Pages. Quickly scan the advertisements there until you feel drawn to a particular company. Focus on this ad and follow your intuition – does this feel like the right company for your move? If so, ring up and make the booking. If not, keep looking until you find a company you feel in your heart will do a good job.

A packing party

Faced with a house move, most of us find ourselves wondering how we have managed to collect so much stuff. Packing is usually an exhausting experience. If you have a family, you've probably accumulated masses of belongings over the years, and the children's rooms alone may easily take a few days to pack! As daunting as all this may seem, if you are moving house, there is no avoiding it. However, there is a way to make packing more fun and to spread the workload. What am I referring to? A packing party, of course. This can be a great way to get your life boxed up and ready to go in next to no time! It's also a fabulous way to say your goodbyes to neighbours – and friends too if you are relocating to another part of the country or even emigrating.

Before your guests arrive, you will need to gather everything you need, so make sure you have lots of boxes, packing tape, bubble wrap, sticky labels and marker pens. Then, of course, as you'll be packing all your crockery up, you'll need paper plates and disposable cups, along with a range of ready-made party foods and nibbles. Bottles of wine or juice and perhaps a bottle of champagne will add to the party atmosphere, though too much alcohol may result in breakages, so be moderate. Ask one of your guests to bring a portable CD player and a selection of music. Then, once everyone has arrived, start packing! Delegate different rooms or areas to different people and ask them to name and label each box as it is filled, for example 'kitchen, crockery', 'study, books' and so on. This will make unpacking a lot easier when you arrive in your new home.

Spell to ward possessions from breakage and loss

Once your things are all safely wrapped and packed in boxes, you should magically safeguard them from disaster so that they arrive in one piece at your new home.

What you need
A silver pen, a potion of rock-salt and spring water

What you do
⭐ Using the silver pen, draw a pentagram (or five-pointed star) on each of the boxes.
⭐ Splash all the boxes with the salt and water potion, as you do so, saying:

> *Protected be, protected be,*
> *Until we reach our destiny.*

Spell to cleanse and bless the old house

Not only is it polite to clean the house before you leave, but it is also a magical way of ending that phase of your life and will banish you and your energies from the property. In this way you are leaving a clean slate, both physically and psychically. This will make the property ready for the new tenants and will also help you to detach from the old house – which will, in turn, make it easier for you to settle into your new home.

What you need
A smudge stick or a stick of your favourite incense

What you do

- ⭐ First, clean the house thoroughly – you could even make this a part of your packing party.
- ⭐ Light the smudge stick or incense and go around the house, smudging, or smoking, every room. As you do so, visualise the house filling with blessings for the new tenants. Also use this opportunity to say a silent thank you to the house – it has sheltered you, harboured you and protected you, possibly for many years, so acknowledge this fact.

Leaving magical gifts

An old tradition when leaving a house is to leave a silver coin on the window sill. This will be found by the new residents and will bring prosperity and good fortune to the house itself. Magical people often take this tradition one step further, leaving magical gifts in the garden for the land devas, food for the wildlife and a small silver charm or crystal in the house for the new residents.

What you need

A stick of incense, a suitable plant for planting outside, a clear quartz crystal, a birdseed cake that can be hung outdoors, a small silver pentagram, a rose quartz crystal

What you do

- ⭐ Light the stick of incense and take it outside, along with the plant, clear quartz crystal and birdseed cake. Stake the incense into the garden.
- ⭐ Plant the plant nearby, with the crystal beneath it, as you do so, saying:

  For the land devas and household spirits. I give blessings and thanks. Blessed be!

- ⭐ Hang the birdseed cake from a tree, hedge or even a washing line, as you do so, saying:

For the wildlife of this garden and land. I give blessings and thanks. Blessed be!

⭐ Go back into the house and place the pentagram and rose quartz crystal on an upstairs window sill, as you do so, saying:

For the future residents of this property, with much love and luck to you, whoever you may be. Blessed be!

You are now free to start your new life in your new home.

Moving in

We now come to the most exciting part – moving in! A new home generally means a new start, so the move will probably fill you with eager anticipation.

There are many things you can do to enhance your move magically. An ancient tradition states that the first things to be taken into a new home should be salt (for prosperity), bread (so that you never know hunger) and water or red wine (for the sacred life force). Taking these three items into your home first will ensure that your future there is bright and that you will be well provided for.

Another ancient rite involved taking a glowing ember from the fire of the old house and using it to light the first fire in the new home. In these days of central heating, you can observe this tradition by burning half a tea-light in the old house and then relighting it and allowing it to burn down in your new home.

It's also a good idea to take a cutting from the old garden with you and plant this in your new garden. This will encourage continuity of growth and expansion. Of course, if your herb garden is in pots, or you have a passion for house plants, transporting these to the new home will in itself honour this traditional rite.

One of the first things you should do after moving in is to introduce yourself to the house. You may feel a little silly doing this, but think how important a home is to you and what this house will come to mean to you in the long term. After all, you wouldn't ignore a potential new friend, so don't ignore the soul of your new house. Simply light a candle, say hello and introduce yourself and your family. Ask that the house provide protection and shelter for you and yours, and state that in return you will maintain the house and garden and create a beautiful and magical home.

Ritual to attune with the devas and spirits

This little ritual will help you to attune with the land devas and household spirits around you in your new home. You will need to work it twice, once indoors and once in the garden.

What you need
A tea-light in a suitable holder, a clear quartz crystal, a stick of your favourite incense

What you do
- ✪ Choose a spot for your ritual and go and sit quietly there for at least ten minutes, connecting with the new energies that now surround you. Breathe deeply and close your eyes. Feel your new environment around you, hear the new sounds and breathe in the fragrance of a different air.
- ✪ Light the tea-light and the stick of incense, and take up the quartz crystal in your hands. Hold it gently and say:

> *I call to the devas of this land/household spirits. My name is —.*
> *I have come to share this sacred space with you and I ask for*
> *your assistance in my household magic. Please welcome me to*
> *this place and I shall be a guardian of this home for as long as*
> *it pleases the powers that be. Accept this crystal as a sign of this*
> *pledge and my friendship. Blessed be!*

- ✪ Place the crystal in the soil if you are outdoors, or in a plant pot if you are indoors, and sit for a few moments longer.
- ✪ When you feel the time is right, end the ritual by blowing out the candle and allowing the incense to burn down. Go about your day, knowing that you have begun to create magic in your new home. Don't forget to repeat the spell either indoors or outdoors to complete the attunement.

A magical house-warming party

The best way to bless your new home and fill it with positive energies is to have a party! The traditional house-warming party is an example of how magic has been integrated into modern life – to such an extent that it is rarely regarded as magic any more. But the very phrase 'house warming' has the ring of true magic and witchcraft about it.

Take these magical roots into account when you plan your own house-warming party. A magical theme such as lucky black cats will help to set the mood, as will decorations of silver stars and crescent moons. Alternatively, go for a seasonal theme, or copy the fabled witch's cottage look. Invite all your friends, old and new, and invoke the pixies to make sure your house warming goes with a swing! Your new home will soon be rocking with laughter and jumping to the beat of true earth magic.

Protection Spells

We end this book with a chapter dedicated to protection magic. It is important that you feel safe and secure in your own home, and the spells and rituals of this section are designed to enable you to do just that. However, in order for protection magic to be effective, you must also back it up with sensible security procedures in the mundane world. This means fitting door-chains, spy-holes, dead-bolts, alarms and so on, and making sure you lock doors and windows. Magic can and will protect you and help to keep you safe, but it should always be used in conjunction with good common sense.

Protection rituals should be performed on a regular basis. In fact, most witches operate on the premise that prevention is better than cure, so rather than waiting until we are actually in danger to work a spell, we perform rites daily to ensure that we are never in danger. That is the foundation of good protection magic.

We have looked at very basic protection rituals, such as the warding of doors and windows, throughout the course of this book; here we will be considering protection magic in a little more depth, making use of stronger spells and rituals. But first let's take a look at how you can enhance your warrior spirit ...

Warrior spirit

'Warrior spirit' is a term I have been using for years with regard to my own life. I have noticed that I draw strength and courage from many different sources, such as nature, myths and legends, history, magic, my ancestry and so on. This has led me to believe that courage is a tangible energy and that we can summon and tap into it whenever we need to. This is the warrior spirit. Like magic, it comes from within but can also be invoked. We all have the warrior spirit within us; it is a gift from the witches' god, or from the higher powers that be.

Let me clarify here that a warrior isn't necessarily a man! History offers many female warriors to encourage and inspire us girls – think of feisty females such as Boudicca, Joan of Arc and Pocohontas, for example. Anyone can be a warrior, regardless of gender!

Another point that should be clarified is that being in tune with your warrior spirit does not mean indulging in random violence. A true warrior knows that the strongest weapon is the brain and that the greatest chance of victory lies in keeping a cool head and maintaining a calm yet strong attitude to any adversity.

You have a tremendous source of courage, power and strength within you, and you can use this warrior spirit to help you through the toughest times. All you need to do in order to tap into it is to realise that it's there. Acknowledge your power right now, summoning it by saying:

> I am a warrior. I have the warrior spirit within me. I can win through all the battles of my life. So mote it be!

Combine this strength with protection spells, magical knowledge and a positive attitude, and you will soon become a force truly to be reckoned with!

Thought forms

As the name suggests, a thought form is a thought or visualisation that you have given shape and form to. This energy field is then directed to do your bidding. Thought forms are one of the most powerful and adaptable forms of protection magic you can create. They are an extension of your psychic powers, and you can give them any shape you wish. Thus you can create astral dragons, unicorns, vampires, wolves and so on to protect you and your property. If your thought form is powerful enough, it may even be perceived by others as a kind of ghost.

Just recently my mother felt that she needed a little protection magic around her, and asked me to work with her to cast a spell. We decided to use the Wolf Protection Spell from my book *The Witch's Almanac*. We said the spell together over the phone, and just as we finished I felt a surge of power leave me from my heart chakra. It was as though I had been kicked in the chest by a horse! I had never cast a spell with another witch over a distance before, and, I must admit, I was totally unprepared for this! Then, seconds later, my mother felt the power arrive. Though we didn't discuss how we would visualise the wolf thought form, we both saw it in our mind's eye as being in the same place. This was a very strong magical connection between two witches, and the thought form that we created was very powerful.

Creating a thought form of protection

What you need
Your athame (optional)

What you do

⭐ First of all, decide what form you wish to create – this should be something that makes you feel safe and protected. Popular choices are wolves, dragons, angels and dark shadowy figures.

⭐ Once you have the shape in your mind, draw an outline of it in the air before you, using your athame or your finger. This outline should be as life-sized as you can make it – or, alternatively, you can imagine it growing in size once you've finished the drawing.

⭐ Clearly visualise your chosen image and blow three times into the outline you have created. This will effectively breathe life into your thought form.

⭐ You can now command the thought form to protect you, your home, your car, your pet and so on. Just remember to acknowledge the thought form daily to keep the power strong.

Wiccan protection prayer

This little ritual will enhance your feeling of safety when you are asleep, and thus at your most vulnerable.

What you do

⭐ Each night, before going to sleep, say the following prayer:

> *Hail to the Great Mother Goddess! I ask that you protect*
> *me and my loved ones, my pets, and my home and property.*
> *Protect me and mine from all harm, seen and unseen,*
> *worldly and otherworldly, elemental, accidental and*
> *criminal. This is my plea. So mote it be! Blessed be!*

Circle of salt

Salt is used by witches for purification and protection. The following spell is a traditional rite of protection.

What you need
A tub of rock-salt

What you do

⭐ Use the rock-salt to create a circle around the perimeter of your home. If you cannot completely encircle your home, visualise the salt circle continuing around the areas that you cannot access. As you work, focus your energies on your home remaining completely safe from all negativity and any who mean you harm.

⭐ Once you have completed your circle, say:

> *Protected be!*

Your spell is done.

Spell to turn back negativity

This spell is worked in the mind's eye, and can be used effectively anywhere to protect anything. However, you can enhance the spell by hanging a small mirror outside your home or on the dashboard of your car. Crystals can be used to the same effect and are a little more discreet.

What you do

⊛ Imagine yourself, your home, your vehicle or whatever needs protection as being surrounded by a circle of mirrors. These mirrors face outwards and will reflect all negativity back to the sender.

⊛ Say the following chant, either out loud or in your head:

Turn back negativity to whence it came;
This I command, in witchcraft's name.

Spell to turn back gossip

When we are forced to live in close proximity to others, there are bound to be personality clashes. Add to this the fact that some witches have to suffer prejudice on a daily basis and you may end up with a gossip problem on your hands. If people are talking about you, for whatever reason, try this spell to protect yourself from their spite.

What you need

Your athame (or a vegetable knife), a gingerbread man, a length of black ribbon, a circle of cooking foil about the size of a two-pence piece

What you do

⊛ Take everything you need to your main altar. Using your athame or the vegetable knife, inscribe the name of the gossip on the tummy of the gingerbread man. If you don't know the name, use the house number or simply the word 'gossips'.

⊛ Tie the ribbon tightly around the mouth of the gingerbread man so that it is symbolically gagged. This will stop the gossip talking about you.

⊛ Glue the foil circle over the gagged mouth to reflect all negative speech back to the gossip.

⊛ Bury the gingerbread man in your garden or at a crossroads, as you do so, saying:

Hide the gossip from the light;
Circle of silver, turn back spite.
Small of mind brings gift of woe;
The hurt they cause, they soon shall know.

Spell to detach a property

If you live in a flat or even in a terraced house, you can sometimes feel a little hemmed in, and you may pick up on and be affected by negativity from other homes around you. A great way to separate your home from all the rest is to create a magic circle around it. This will effectively detach your home from the others by magic, protecting it from any unhelpful energies that may be lingering around; as a result you will feel a healthy separation from the neighbours and the homes around you. Repeat the spell on a daily basis. It takes only a moment to perform, but within a week you should begin to notice a difference in the atmosphere of your home.

What you need
Your athame (optional)

What you do
⭐ Stand in the middle of your home and, holding your athame (or your index finger) outstretched, turn three times in a deosil (clockwise) direction. As you do so, visualise a stream of beautiful rose-coloured light creating a pink bubble all around your flat or house. As well as detaching your home, this will also protect it and fill it with magic and love.

Spell to protect your garden

This spell is a variation on the triple circle-casting of witchcraft. It should be performed on the full moon and repeated every few months.

What you need
4 tea-lights and appropriate lanterns, a compass (optional)

What you do

- ⭐ Walk the boundary of your garden to define the space.
- ⭐ Go around again, this time placing a lantern and an unlit tea-light at each cardinal point (north, south, east and west). If you need to, use the compass for this.
- ⭐ Make a third and final trip around the circle, this time lighting each tea-light. As you do so, say:

  Protected be!

Allow the tea-lights to burn themselves out, making sure that, for safety, you keep an eye on them.

Spell to protect a door

If there is a room in your house that you wish to keep safe from the prying eyes of visitors, use this old witch trick. It's great for protecting a temple or altar room, or even just the mess of a junk room!

What you need
A traditional witch's broomstick

What you do

- ⭐ Place the broomstick slant ways across the door of the room you want to protect. The brush of the broom should be to the east and the handle to the west, so following the path of the sun.
- ⭐ Hold your hands out to the broom, as you do so, saying:

  Protect this door from those who pry;
  Keep this room hidden from intrusive eyes.
  May the power of this witch's broom
  Keep safe the secrets of this room.
  So mote it be!

Spell for angelic protection

For a strong and loving protection, invoke the powers of your guardian angel. I wrote this spell several years ago, and it is one of my personal favourites. If you can, memorise the invocation so that you can call on angel power whenever you have need of it, at any time and in any place.

What you need
A white candle and a suitable holder

What you do
- ✪ Light the candle and bring the image of an angel to mind. When you are ready, speak the following invocation:

> *Guardian angel, bring your light;*
> *Make my future days as bright.*
> *Bring with you an angelic shield,*
> *As your mighty sword you wield.*
> *Embrace me with protective wings;*
> *Guard me from all harmful things.*
> *I call you here your power to lend*
> *And welcome the love of an angel friend.*

Spell to gain protection from unwelcome visitors

What you need
Equal parts of black pepper, turmeric, garlic powder and dried bergamot

What you do
- ✪ Sprinkle the mixture of herbs and spices on your threshold every day, as you do so, saying:

> *Those whom I do not wish to see*
> *Are kept away by the powers that be.*

Spell to protect your car

Remember to back this spell up by locking your car each time you leave it and placing all valuables in the boot. You should also install an alarm and use a crook lock.

What you need
A white candle in a sturdy holder, your athame or another inscribing tool, your pentacle, an amethyst crystal

What you do
- Using your athame or other inscribing tool, inscribe the registration number of your car on to the candle.
- Place the candle, in the holder, on top of your pentacle. Place the amethyst crystal (for protection) on the pentacle too, just in front of the candle. Now imagine your vehicle being engulfed in a circle of brilliant white light.
- With this visualisation clear in your mind, light the candle to begin the magic, allowing it to burn down naturally.
- Place the amethyst crystal in the glove compartment of your car.

Chant for protection while driving

The first thing I noticed after passing my driving test was how much hostility there is on today's roads. It came as a bit of a shock to see how inconsiderate some drivers are of their own and other people's safety. To increase my feeling of safety (not to mention improve my chances of survival) I decided to create a simple protection chant that could be said before setting off on any journey, however short. This is what I came up with – feel free to change and adapt it to your own needs:

> *Goddess and angels, protect me now. Let me drive safely,*
> *carefully and with harm to none. Guide my vehicle from harm's*
> *way and bring me and my car back home safe and sound.*
> *So mote it be!*

Afterword

Within this book I have set out to illustrate how simple hearth magic can be and to show you how, with just a little thought and a bit of effort, any home can become a magical one. The hedge witches of old did not have complex rituals, elaborate robes and expensive ritual tools to hand. Instead they had the power of natural magic at their fingertips, and they worked within the confines of their own house and garden.

I hope that this book has inspired you to turn your own home into a magical sanctuary and to view it as your personal covenstead. Remember that magic is all around you, and you can tap into it at any time. By putting the magic back into your home you are taking a vital step towards self-empowerment and will see your life begin to change for the better.

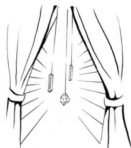

Magic should not be separate from daily life; on the contrary, it should be an intrinsic part of our daily routine, thus filling each day with enchantment. By performing daily magical household chores such as warding doors and windows, attuning with Vesta, and blessing the food we cook and eat, we are connecting our modern life with the ancient power of the witch's way. This in turn will help us to lead an even more charmed life.

As I have been writing this book, my thoughts have often turned to those unfortunate people who do not have the luxury of a home. Please spare a thought for homeless people – and if you can, spare some change! Buying a copy of the *Big Issue* or making a small donation to a charity such as Shelter, Crisis or St Mungo's not only offers a helping hand to those who are down on their luck, but also affirms your gratitude that you have a home to call your own. Remember that what we give out (including our spare change) comes back to us times three. So that's three good reasons to be charitable!

May you continue to create and enjoy your soul home. Make it beautiful, make it magical, and when life gets tough, tap your ruby-slippered heels together and say:

There's no place like home, there's no place like home ...

Farewell, my magical reader. Hold fast to your dreams, for they are the reflection of all your tomorrows. May your gods go with you, until our next merry meeting.

Blessed be!

Morgana

Index